# LGBT+ STUDIES IN TURKEY

# LGBT+ STUDIES IN TURKEY

Edited by

## Çağlar Özbek

CONTRIBUTORS:

Ayçin Alp

Sinan Aşçı

Erhan Aydın

Selin Berghan

İdil Engindeniz

Evrim Ersöz Koç

Yasemin Giritli İnceoğlu

Nazan Maksudyan

Çağlar Özbek

Mustafa F. Özbilgin

Gaye Gökalp Yılmaz

TRANSNATIONAL PRESS LONDON

2019

LGBT+ STUDIES IN TURKEY
Edited by Çağlar Özbek

First Published in 2019 by TRANSNATIONAL PRESS LONDON in the United Kingdom, 12 Ridgeway Gardens, London, N6 5XR, UK.
www.tplondon.com

Transnational Press London® and the logo and its affiliated brands are registered trademarks.

Requests for permission to reproduce material from this work should be sent to: sales@tplondon.com

Paperback
ISBN: 978-1-912997-11-4

Cover Design: Gizem Çakır
Cover Image: The Portrait of Taner Ceylan 1, oil on canvas, 34×54, 2002, by Taner Ceylan (We are grateful for permission).

www.tplondon.com

# ABOUT THE AUTHORS

**Ayçin Alp** is a lecturer in Avrasya University, Department of Social Security. Currently she is PhD student and completed her master's degree in Muğla Sıtkı Koçman University Department of Sociology. Her Master thesis 'Türkiye'de Dezavantajlı Grupların Mesleki Hayata Katılımları: İstanbul'da LGBTİ Bireyler', besides being worked on the sociology of cinema. Her areas of interest are disadvantages groups, LGBTIQ, social policy and security.

**Sinan Aşçı** received his Bachelors degree in English Language Teaching in 2010 from Anadolu University, and took one-year education as an exchange student in British and American Studies at the University of Pardubice in Czech Republic. He then shifted his academic focus towards media and journalism, and completed a Masters degree in General Journalism at Marmara University in 2013. His thesis work focused on the representation of LGBT individuals in newspapers in Turkey and the States. He earned a Ph.D. in Media and Communication Studies with a thesis work mainly focusing on "cyberbullying and youth in Turkey" under the supervision of Dr. Michel Bourse from Galatasaray University in 2018. He has been teaching media courses at associate and undergraduate level in Turkey and Germany, and doing research on social media, digital journalism, and digital literacy. He is a full-time faculty member in the Department of New Media at Bahçeşehir University, and working with an international research team as a PDRA for SDI München with a focus on "building social research capacities in HEIs.

**Erhan Aydın** is an Assistant Prof. of Management and Organization in Usak University, Turkey. He earned his PhD in Brunel Business School, Brunel University London and MSc in Dokuz Eylul University, Turkey. He also was Recognized Visiting Researcher at Said Business School, University of Oxford from 2016 to 2017. He has three bachelor degrees in the fields of Business Administration, International Relations and Public Administration. His research interests include diversity, equality and inclusion at organisations, HRM and e-HRM. He is acting as a member of Academy of Management and European Academy of Management. He is amongst the reviewers of Gender, Work & Organization, Gender in Management: An International Journal, Journal of Organizational Change Management (Editorial Advisory Board Member) and Personnel Review. His research has been published in well- known publication houses such as Sage and Edward Elgar, and journals such as Journal of Organizational Change Management.

**Selin Berghan** graduated from the department of sociology at the Hacettepe University in 2002, then got her masters' degree from the same department in 2004. Her masters' thesis was published as a book with the title of "Lubunya: Trans Kimlik ve Beden" (Lubunya: Trans Identity and

i

Body) by Metis Publishing House in 2007. This study is still the only academic research published on trans identity in Turkey. She has actively participated in trans activism, and also worked as a board member of the Pembe Hayat, first and only trans lead organization in Turkey. At the same time, she worked in the field of children's rights, specifically in the area of children in conflict with law. She produced several reports and documents on violence against children, child protection, and refugee children for some national and international organizations such as UNICEF, ICC. She is currently working in the Civil Society Development Centre within a European Union Programme for strengthening civil society in the candidate countries. Her studies and works on the transfeminism and children's rights are available in this address: www.selinberghan.com (in Turkish).

**İdil Engindeniz** is research assistant at Galatasaray University, Faculty of Communication, where she also studied journalism. She got her master degree and her PhD in France, at Université Stendhal, Grenoble 3, on communications. For her PhD, she worked about the LGBT movement in Turkey and the LGBT public sphere, focusing especially on Kaos GL and its magazine. Her research areas are public sphere, journalism, communication ethics, LGBTI studies, gender studies.

**Evrim Ersöz Koç** is an Assistant Professor in the Department of American Culture and Literature at Dokuz Eylül University in İzmir. She received her PhD degree in 2011 with a dissertation on the representations of apocalypse in the contemporary American drama. Her research interests include mainly American drama and American cinema.

**Yasemin Giritli İnceoğlu** professor of journalism, member of the UNESCO International Clearinghouse on Children and Violence on the Screen and of the American Biography Institute was a visiting scholar at Columbia University (1994) at the Salzburg Seminar (2003), New Delhi University Media Studies Center (2014) and EUI -European University Institute (2017) and she is one of the founder members of the Media Watch Platform in Turkey (2008). Yasemin İnceoğlu has participated at the second Alliance of Civilizations Conference in Istanbul (2009) and at an international meeting on media literacy organized by UNESCO in Paris (2007). Recently, she took part of a project sponsored by Open Society Foundation, Global Dialogue and Netherlands Consulate General in Istanbul, as a member of the supervisors' board of the Association of Social Change on "Hate Crimes in the Turkish National Press". Dr. Yasemin İnceoğlu is also in the Advisory Board of ASULIS –Hate speech Laboratory of Hrant Dink Foundation. She has published several books: The Persuasion Process in Communications: With Some Examples of the Political Campaigns (1997); Media and Society, Women in the Media and Women Journalists (2002); International Media (2004); A Guide to Media and Children (2008); Text Analysis (2009); Women and their Body in the Spiral of Femininity, Sexuality and Violence (2010),

Hate Speech and Hate Crimes (2012) Minorities, The Other and Media (2014), Internet and Street (2015) News Readings(2016) Her areas of studies are International media, war and the media, persuasive communication and hate speech. She teaches Alternative Media and Journalism Rights, Communication Ethics, International Communication International Communication and Theories and Models of Communication.

**Nazan Maksudyan** is Einstein guest professor at the Friedrich-Meinecke-Institut at the Freie Universität Berlin and a research associate at the Centre Marc Bloch (Berlin). She was a "Europe in the Middle East – The Middle East in Europe" (EUME) Fellow in 2009-10 at the Wissenschaftskolleg zu Berlin and an Alexander von Humboldt Stiftung Postdoctoral Fellow at the Leibniz-Zentrum Moderner Orient (Berlin) in 2010-11 and in 2016-18. From 2013 to 16, she worked as a professor of history in Istanbul and received her habilitation degree in 2015. Her research mainly focuses on the history of children and youth in the Ottoman Empire during the nineteenth and twentieth centuries, with special interest in gender, sexuality, education, humanitarianism, and non-Muslims. Among her publications, *Orphans and Destitute Children in the Late Ottoman Empire* (Syracuse University Press, 2014) is one of the pioneering contributions to the social history of children and youth in the Ottoman Empire. Her edited volume, *Women and the City, Women in the City* (Berghahn, 2014), provided an under-researched gendered lens to Ottoman urban history. Her forthcoming book, *Ottoman Children & Youth During World War I* (2019) adds a new dimension to the historiography of the war by exploring the variegated experiences and involvement of Ottoman children and youth.

**Çağlar Özbek** is an Assistant Professor in Muğla Sıtkı Koçman University, Department of Labor Economics and Industrial Relations. Özbek, completed his PhD at Muğla Sıtkı Koçman University, Department of Sociology with the thesis titled; *"New Actors of Democracy: Non-Governmental Organisations Within the Context of Ecologic, Feminist and LGBT Movements"*. He worked as a research assistant at the same university for 9 years at the Department of Sociology. His interests include international migration, gender, LGBTIQ studies, social movements, citizenship and identity. He is the co-author of the book *Yerlileşen Yabancılar-Güney Ege Bölgesi'nde Göç, Yurttaşlık ve Kimliğin Dönüşümü* (with Muammer Tuna, Detay Publishing). He worked as researcher in various research projects supported by TUBİTAK, EU, UNDP, United States Department of Labor and various organizations.

**Mustafa Özbilgin** is Professor of Organisational Behaviour at Brunel Business School, London. He also holds two international positions: Co-Chaire Management et Diversité at Université Paris Dauphine and Professor of Management at Koç University in Istanbul. His research focuses on equality, diversity and inclusion at work from comparative and rela- tional perspectives. His work has a focus on changing policy and practice of equality and diversity management at work. He served as the editor-in-chief of the *European Management Review* (EMR), the official journal of the European Academy of Management (EURAM)..

**Gaye Gökalp Yılmaz** has received her B.A degree from Bilkent University, Department of Political Science and Public Administration and continued her academic studies at Muğla Sıtkı Koçman University, Department of Sociology. Gökalp Yılmaz has received her M.A degree from Muğla Sıtkı Koçman University, Department of Sociology with the Thesis Titled; Analysis of The Socio- Economic Transformations in Turkey after 1980, with World-Systems Approach. Gökalp Yılmaz continued her Ph.D Studies at Muğla Sıtkı Koçman University, Department of Sociology and received her Ph.D degree with the thesis titled; Everyday Life Sociology and Tactics of Turkish Origin People Living İn Germany: Germany-Aachen Case Study. After receiving her Ph. D. degree, Gökalp Yılmaz has started to work as Faculty Member and Assistant Prof. at Burdur Mehmet Akif Ersoy University, Department of Sociology in 2016. Gökalp Yılmaz still continue her academic studies on Everyday Life Sociology, Social Change, Social Structure in Turkey and Cultural Studies. Gökalp Yılmaz has many publications regarding her academic interests and a book titled; "An Analysis with Michel De Certeau's Everyday Life Sociology: Everyday Life Practices and Tactics of Turks in Germany".

# CONTENTS

PREFACE: WHAT IS GOING ON UNDER THE RAINBOW
Çağlar Özbek .................................................................................. 3


**PART I. THEORETICAL AND EMPIRICAL DEBATES** ............7

CHAPTER 1

EXPLORING THE INTERPLAY BETWEEN THE AIMS AND THE
CONTEXT OF LGBTI+ ORGANISING: THE CASE OF LGBTI+
ORGANISATIONS IN TURKEY AND THE UK
Erhan Aydın and Mustafa F. Özbilgin.................................... 9

CHAPTER 2

A COMPARATIVE LOOK AT LGBT RIGHTS AND
ACQUISITIONS: EUROPEAN UNION AND TURKEY
Gaye Gökalp Yılmaz......................................................... 33

CHAPTER 3

TRANS WOMEN PRISONERS IN TURKEY
Selin Berghan ........................................................................ 47

CHAPTER 4

OTHERS IN MEDIA: LGBT INDIVIDUALS
Yasemin Giritli İnceoğlu ......................................................... 61

CHAPTER 5

SOCIAL MEDIA USE IN LGBTQI MOVEMENTS IN TURKEY
Sinan Aşçı ............................................................................ 65


**PART II. CONTEXTUAL ANALYSIS** .........................................79

CHAPTER 6

QUEER CHARACTERS AND GENDER PERFORMANCES IN
SAIT FAIK'S WORKS
Nazan Maksudyan .................................................................. 81

CHAPTER 7

AN ANALYSIS OF THE CINEMATIC REPRESENTATION OF
LGBT: LOLA AND BILLY THE KID
Ayçin Alp and Çağlar Özbek.................................................... 97

CHAPTER 8

KAOS GL MAGAZINE'S ROLE IN THE EMERGENCE OF THE
LGBTI PUBLIC SPHERE IN TURKEY
İdil Engindeniz ...................................................................... 115

CHAPTER 9

TRANSPHOBIA IN EBRU NİHAN CELKAN'S KİMSENİN
ÖLMEDİĞİ BİR GÜNÜN ERTESİYDİ (AFTER THE DAY
NOBODY DIED)
Evrim Ersöz Koç .................................................................. 131

# PREFACE: WHAT IS GOING ON UNDER THE RAINBOW

Çağlar Özbek

Today, the concept of gender is being re-defined throughout the world. The change that penetrates both the theoretical and the daily life, especially under the leadership of the USA and Europe, is recognised rapidly but with caution most of the time.

Unisex clothes, the world-famous fashion brands employing androgen models in their parades, many Western cultures allowing same-sex marriages and allowing those couples to have (adopt) children imply a genderless social structure. This anti-genderism comes along with the markets that produce even toothpaste or shower gel for women and men separately. The commercials and TV series still exploit the dualist identities of modernity as a marketing feature. The emphasis on violence against the disadvantaged identities is fed here. The alienation, which was once carried out on AIDS, is now carried out on other obscurities today. Transphobia, homophobia, biphobia and other phobia that was fed by heteronormativity is more prominent more than they have ever been.

Here stands the great paradox!

The debates on being a woman and a man in Turkey was followed by the debate on being an LGBT individual in Turkey, in 1980s. During this period, where a new world order was formed, it was not a coincidence that LGBT being a subject of social life, first and academic studies, then. This period, for Turkey, is associated with a rapid rise of capitalism, neo-liberalism, and the post-coup fractions in the society. In this period the NGOs in Turkey began to make themselves heard in LGBT.

In the early 1990s, LGBT organizations started as small initiatives, and later, becoming associations, gained identities. As of 1990, the universities have become aware of LGBT. The universities associating with the NGOs took this movement to an international stage. As of this period the agency not only expanded throughout Turkey but also began to be debated on international stages.

## What is LGBT an Alternative for?

Is it possible that LGBT has emerged as an alternative against the debates

3

on manhood and womanhood, which constitutes the grounds of dualist identities, a discovery of modernity?

This question may stand as an unreasonable one for many. However, in consideration of historical background, it can be seen that in almost all regions of the world, there has been a history on homosexuality. If this unwritten history has been standing as a literary knowledge, then what may have led to emergence of LGBT as a conceptual mark?

What might be the contribution of postmodernity, a relatively liberating theory, against the dualist identities of modernity. No doubt that political attitudes would seek for different responses to this question. However, the "new order" understanding in post-1980 world increased the emphasis on identity policies. This emphasis, without doubt, has deeply influenced gender, which is the most fundamental category of identity. Therefore, this "new order" is considered to be the ground for the sexual orientations other than heterosexuality that have been preferred/forced to remain latent, to speak louder for themselves.

Could there be any LGBT policies that may liberalise sexual orientations in this respect? Why not? LGBT, against the dominance heteronormative speech that considers womanhood and the sense of motherhood equal and making manhood a symbol of power and competence, opens a gate for different sexual orientations as well. This gate has long been counter-forced with great resistance. There are still countries, where homosexuality is considered a crime. On the other hand, there are countries, where such social policies as allowing same-sex marriage and adoption of children by homosexual couples, granting rights to succession and labour have been legalized and practiced.

Considering and following all these developments in the context of human rights, is within the agenda of Turkey, along with the rest of the world.

This volume brings together a selection of discussions on LGBT that are presented from different points of view and from different disciplines. This compilation consisting of nine chapters, focuses on the perspectives on LGBT in Turkey, in a broad range from NGOs to cinema, social policies to theatres.

All chapters discuss Turkey and the studies of LGBT in Turkey and presented in two parts. First part is about the theoric and empirical studies which takes over Turkey experiences from a structural perspective. Still, in this first part, there are two chapters which explain the comparison of UK and EU experiences with Turkey.

The second part has more of text analysis which indicates cultural studies. Also the second part contains text analysis which treads LGBT theme from a specialty for cinema, litarature, theater and magazine. While I was preparing this book, I aim to combine aroud one theme and when this theme is being, I prefer to set free the writers for their studies. Eventually, the LGBT issiue in Turkey has already been in the delimited studies.

In this sense, prison experiences of trans women, represantation of LGBT in cinema and civil society organisations' comparative analysis have the importance which can not be compared to each other.

I am therefore thankful to those have contributed to this book and long waited for it to mature. With this study, I wish you gain different point of views for your own studies, use as an efficient resource and create new paths for the readers.

# PART I.

# THEORETICAL AND EMPIRICAL DEBATES

# CHAPTER 1

# EXPLORING THE INTERPLAY BETWEEN THE AIMS AND THE CONTEXT OF LGBTI+ ORGANISING: THE CASE OF LGBTI+ ORGANISATIONS IN TURKEY AND THE UK

Erhan Aydın and Mustafa F. Özbilgin

*Sexual minority research mostly considers experiences of LGBTI+ individuals at work. However, there is a dearth of studies regarding the role of LGBTI+ organisations in protecting LGBTI+ rights within different national settings from contextual and institutional perspective. For this reason, we explore the interplay between the aims of LGBTI+ organisations and the international, national and institutional contexts in which they operate. Drawing on 40 semi- structured qualitative interviews (20 in each country) with the members of LGBTI+ organisations in Turkey and the UK, the study demonstrates that the organisations in Turkey focus on establishing and legitimating LGBTI+ rights in institutions such as education and work. Whereas the organisations in the UK aim at promoting better conditions of life and work. Drawing on comparative data, we make two critical contributions to the LGBTI+ literature. First, we study two different country settings, which illustrate the context dependence of LGBTI+ organising. Second, we demonstrate the significance of understanding the heterogeneity of aims among LGBTI+ institutions in two different national settings. Our chapter challenges the fundamental assumption that LGBTI+ organisations would share common goals and have similar aims activities. Instead, we demonstrate the interplay of international, national and institutional contexts of LGBTI+ organisations in shaping and differentiating their aims and raison d'etre.*

## Introduction

Studies on Lesbian, Gay, Bisexual, Trans, Intersex and other sexuality (LGBTI+) issues mostly adopt an individual level of analysis that covers discrimination, violence, voice and visibility (Rumens, 2016; McPhail et al., 2016; Yılmaz and Gocmen, 2016; Wright, 2015; Ozturk, 2011; Colgan et al., 2007). For this reason, mainstream research focuses on reporting individual experiences, through a critical and emancipatory paradigm. Yet the mainstream research surprisingly neglects the role of LGBTI+ organisations in protecting and fighting against the individual challenges that LGBTI+ individuals face in both organisations and society. In this chapter, we fill this void by exploring the often underplayed meso level of LGBTI+ issues, i.e. LGBTI+ organisations in their international, national and institutional settings. In particular, we examine the aims of the LGBTI+ organisations, in their particular context.

In order to explore the aims of LGBTI+ organisations, we first focus on LGBTI+ organisations in terms of their legal standing and rights. In this perspective, we consider the legislative framework of Turkey and the UK for diagnosing the current situation. We secondly explore the role that LGBTI+ organisations play in two societies. We examine the interplay of LGBTI+ organisations and social life in order to understand the aims of LGBTI+ organisations in the context of social norms, needs and conditions. We also explore the international context of LGBTI+ organisations and the extent of the role international context play.

The study draws on 40 in-depth semi- structured interviews (20 in each country) with the members of LGBTI+ organisations in Turkey and the UK. All interviews were recorded and transcribed by the first author and Nvivo10 was used to provide data categorisation for our study.

We make three critical contributions to the LGBTI+ literature. First, we study two different country settings which illustrate the context dependence of LGBTI+ activism; and second, we demonstrate the significance of understanding the heterogeneity of aims among LGBTI+ institutions in two different national settings.

This book chapter divided into five sections. In the first section, we explicate the legal rights of LGBTI+ and their organisations in Turkey and the UK. Secondly, we consider them in the social context through an exploration of norms and values in each country. Third, we introduce the research methods. Fourth, we report the findings in Turkey and the UK, respectively. Then, we conclude our study and provide future research directions.

## THE LEGAL CONTEXT OF LGBTI+ INDIVIDUALS AND THE LGBTI+ ORGANISATIONS IN TURKEY AND THE UK

The constitution of Turkey, principally, suggests that all citizens are equal in front of the law regardless of their sex, ethnicity, language, political and religious understanding (Duman et al., 2016). The constitution, however, does not state any specific articles regarding equality of sexual orientation or preventing discrimination against sexual minorities (Oner, 2015). For this reason, the constitution as a major law of Turkey does not have any argument for both the prohibition or protection of LGBTI+ individuals or their relationships. This situation indicates that the legal system of Turkey is silent on the subject of discrimination against LGBTI+ individuals in social life. However, this silence de facto means that LGBTI+ individuals face problems in social, economic and political spheres because there are rules and procedures, which have dire consequences for LGBTI+ individuals. The main challenge against equality for LGBTI+ individuals comes from traditional structure and norms in society, which consider LGBTI+ individuals as a challenge to "the morals of society" and have "unnatural sexual behaviour" (International Helsinki Federation for Human Rights, 2006 cited in Yurtsever and Erdoğan, 2010).

Even though there are no explicit statements regarding LGBTI+ individuals in the constitutions or the laws in Turkey, individuals, public servants, legal bodies and judges, who interpret laws often consider same-sex relationships as "immoral and dishonourable behaviour" (e.g. Article 125 of Civil Servants Law). For instance, The High Discipline Board of the Ministry of the Interior made a decision for dismissing a police officer on 20 April 2004 due to the evidence of his having engaged in sexual intercourse with his same-sex partner. The decision of this board was based on Article 125 of Civil Servants Law (no: 657) which states that "to act in an immoral and dishonourable way, which is not compatible with the position of a civil servant" (Amnesty International, 2011: 23). Consequently, this case, among many others, sets precedents for and exposes the legal basis for discriminative practices against LGBTI+ individuals who work in the public sector.

In addition to the public sector, lack of protection with regards to employment of LGBTI+ individuals in the private sector causes the dismissal of employees without being given any particular reason by employers. LGBTI+, however, mostly feel that it is due to their sexual orientation, which is visible in their life (Amnesty International, 2011). The research of Ozturk (2011) which focuses on discrimination at work in the context of Turkey revealed specific cases in order to point out how discrimination occurs in the context of Turkey. One of the cases describes the experience of a gay employee whose sexual orientation was uncovered by one of his colleagues. The employee was subsequently fired by the employer a day after with summary dismissal. Such experiences highlight the uncomfortable and closeted context in which LGBTI+ individuals operate in the workplace (Amnesty International, 2011: 23).

Due to the dearth of protective legislation, there are cases of discrimination against LGBTI+ individuals in both the public and private sectors in Turkey. LGBTI+ individuals, however, seek solidarity and freedom by organising around their common priorities under LGBTI+ institutions which are in the form of NGOs in Turkey. Creating LGBTI+

NGOs is merely made possible by the decree that people have the freedom to establish an association without the permission of any legal authorities (5253 Associations Law, 2004).

The freedom of founding an association in practice, however, is limited because of given reasons such as public morality and family values. Thereby, even though forming an association is a legitimate right for individuals, the understandings of morality and values have been used in a discriminative manner for LGBTI+ organisations in Turkey. This way of approaching LGBTI+ organisations brings to request the closure of LGBTI+ organisations. For instance, The Youth and Ecology Association (Turkish: Gençlik ve Ekoloji Derneği) was on trial because of its practices with regard to LGBTI+ individuals, which was interpreted as being against Turkish laws and morality. The association, however, won the case against the governorate (Kaos GL, 2014). All these cases that are mentioned in this section have been stated towards legislative and regulative misinterpretations. The lack of legislations and misinterpretations of regulations constitute significant obstacles for LGBTI+ both in society and in organisations in order to survive in a society and legal system which does not have a flair for non-conformist organising or protest movements. As such the LGBTI+ NGOs in Turkey are forced to remain within the constraints of public morality which are very narrowly defined by law and social mores in Turkey.

In the UK context, on the other hand, the LGBTI+ movement has made significant progress in terms of individual, partnership and organising rights for LGBTI+ individuals. Thus, the legal rights provided both visibility in the public sphere and an inclusive environment for LGBTI+ individuals and organisations. During the rule of the Labour Government between 1997 and 2010, the government increased the promotion of equality and social inclusion through legislations, such as the introduction of the Employment Equality Regulations (2003), which considers sexual orientation as a diversity, which prohibits discrimination on the grounds of sexual orientation, the Gender Recognition Act (2004), the Civil Partnership Act (2004), and the Equality Act (2007; 2010). Introduction of progressive laws on equality for LGBTI+ individuals created an inclusive environment across multiple domains of life such as the workplace, family and media.

Following the prohibition of discrimination on the grounds of sexual orientation through legislations, the number of written organisational policies which support LGBTI+ equality increased (Kersley et al., 2013). Furthermore, The Employment Equality Regulations (2003) with Civil Partnership Act (2004) and the Equality Act (2007) which focus on combatting discrimination against LGBTI+ individuals strengthened the rights of LGBTI+ individuals in the UK (Colgan and Wright, 2011).

Legislative framework in the UK aims at protecting LGBTI+ rights in every institution of society. According to Colgan and Wright (2011), legal and constitutional amendments such as The Equality Act, which prohibits discrimination against LGBTI+s, created opportunities for sexual orientation equality in the UK. Legal protection, however, does not necessarily secure LGBTI+ inclusiveness in organisations (Colgan et al., 2007). In addition, progressive organisations such as those which identify themselves as LGBTI+ friendly in order to attract talented LGBTI+ individuals as employees or customers, promoted LGBTI+ friendly practices. Such progressive organisational practices were more instrumental than written statements alone in promoting and widening access to sexual orientation equality (Colgan and Wright, 2011; Tatli, 2011). For instance, when an LGBTI+ employee invites a partner to an organisation's event, it might be more meaningful than a formal equality statement.

Based on the documentary analysis of the reports of LGBTI+ organisations such as Stonewall in the UK, Aydin (2017) demonstrated that LGBTI+ people still face discrimination even though regulations and legislations, and formal equality statements of organisations have LGBTI+ friendly discourses. Aydin (2017) explained that disagreements between LGBTI+ individuals and their companies, even those that have positive LGBTI+ discourses in formal equality statements, may result in further discrimination of LGBTI+, if interpretation of policies do not observe the positive spirit of the policy. For this reason, both discourses and practices are equally important with regard to achieving an inclusive organisational environment for LGBTI+ employees.

## LGBTI+ ORGANISATIONS IN SOCIETY

Absence of equality legislation remains barrier for LGBTI+ NGOs in Turkey to achieve equality, to combat violence, abuse, bullying and discrimination on the grounds of sexual orientation. Inclusiveness in social values and norms are also equally important in order to progress LGBTI+ equality in Turkey, where heterosexuality is still widely assumed as the social norm and overt diversions from the heterosexual norm are socially disapproved (Ozturk, 2011). In order to have insights regarding cultural values and attitudes in relation to homosexuality in Turkey, we have scrutinised World Values Survey (WVS) results in "tolerance to others". The WVS adopts a scale, which is called the Emory Bogardus' social distance that provides a tolerance measurement in society. The scale weighs who respondents would not like to have as their next-door neighbour. According to the results of WVS (2011), 85.4% of participants in Turkey stated that they would not like to have LGBTI+ individuals as neighbours.

Even though there were other categories within the undesirable groups such as drug addicts, different races, immigrants, different religions, unmarried couples living together, LGBTI+ individuals were emphasised as the least desirable group. The results demonstrate that the tolerance of society towards LGBTI+ individuals is at a low level due to the fact that LGBTI+ individuals are seen as "others" in the society. For this reason, creating legislation or making regulations for sexual orientation equality is an important yet insufficient conditions for achieving sexual orientation equality. Changes in social norms and mores in relation to LGBTI+ issues are required in order for true equality to be achieved in Turkish society (Ozturk, 2011). In the same vein, based on Gelfand's (2011) study of cross-cultural analysis where social norms are strong and little tolerance exists for deviance from such norms, Turkey was classified as one of the societies which manifests culturally tight attributes. The socio-cultural background of Turkey shows that LGBTI+ individuals have been considered as engaging in deviant behaviour in society and, accordingly, LGBTI+ individuals, if uncovered or if they out themselves, are marginalised by society.

One of the major problems that LGBTI+ individuals in Turkey face is the lack of legislations and regulations regarding them; because being LGBTI+ in Turkey means in some cases such as the Military Law 1111 that LGBTI+ individuals are considered to have biologically/psychosexually unfit for service (Tahaoglu, 2015). For this reason, in such a socio-cultural background that has support from legislations which provide legitimacy of discrimination, suppression and violence against LGBTI+ have been legitimised through social practices. These dynamics that reveal and even reproduce and consolidate hegemonic masculinity and compulsory heterosexuality, which are deeply rooted and embedded in the life course of an individual across his or her encounters with institutions of significance such as the family, education, military, media, health care, justice and workplace (Ozturk and Ozbilgin, 2015).

Sexual minorities in the UK, on the other hand, have various rights, including civil partnership, same-sex marriage and formal equality in the organisations. Despite the civil rights movement, well-established equality legislations, regulations and protective measures; LGBTI+ individuals still face subtle discrimination such as verbal and homophobic harassment, jokes, and disparagement that includes homosexual content (Aydin, 2017). The report of Stonewall (2013:8) describes the discrimination as follows:

> *Many political parties' own lesbian, gay and bisexual supporters believe they would face discrimination if they were to seek selection as a parliamentary candidate. More than half (52 percent) of gay Conservative Party supporters say they would face barriers in their own party, compared with almost a quarter (23 percent) of gay Labour Party supporters and one in five (20 per cent) gay Liberal Democrat Supporters.*

LGBTI+ individuals, however, gain visibility in society through advances in social and cultural circumstances. Sociological research (e.g. Giuffre et al., 2008) emphasises the social changes based on the acceptance of LGBTI+ individuals in organisations, and Rumens and Broomfield (2014: 366) state that these changes create an environment, which constitutes "identifying genders and plurality of sexuality". As a result of social and cultural progress attained, the collective voice of LGBTI+ individuals through activism in LGBTI+ organisations has witnessed an upsurge in the last three decades in the UK.

Due to the emergence of LGBTI+ support and network groups in organisations and trade unions, social changes helped to increase the voice of LGBTI+. According to the findings of Colgan and McKearney (2012), which is based on qualitative research on LGBTI+ individuals and their allies in 14 work organisations, demonstrate the role of LGBTI+ organisations in making a significant contribution to visibility, voice and activism for LGBTI+ individuals. For this reason, the LGBTI+ organisations have been considered as important actors, which shape and drive sexual orientation equality agenda (Colgan and McKearney, 2012).

Yet, the research of Rumens and Broomfield (2012) demonstrates that LGBTI+ individuals as are still stigmatised with mental illness, which remains a pernicious and common social construct in the UK. Earlier, Goffman (1963b) and Weeks (1995) had documented the detrimental consequences of stigmatisation of LGBTI+ individuals in the UK. Stigmatisation refers to a process a group, e.g. LGBTI+, is socially marked with a negative quality with negative consequences for the members of the group. Stigmatisation and negative stereotyping of LGBTI+ have dire consequences for LGBTI+ individuals such as job losses, bullying, and negative performance outcomes (Bowring and Brewis, 2009).

As outlined above the LGBTI+ organisations in Turkey and the UK have different concerns and priorities that emanate from differences in local needs. In Turkey, main struggle for LGBTI+ organisations is to achieve legal legitimacy and fair interpretation of laws and policies. For this to happen, Turkey needs stepwise cultural change towards more inclusion and equality. It is hopeful that LGBTI+ organisations now have long history despite a relatively confrontational national context. The case of the UK is different where supportive legal and social context is emerging. Yet the LGBTI+ organisations also identify barriers to effective inclusion of LGBTI+ individuals across all facades of social and political life. For both countries, the LGBTI+ organisations seek legitimacy in social and national context by engaging with current frameworks of law and social norms and mores. It is evident in both countries that the engagement with political context in the country needs attention as the current political regimes appear less interested in LGBTI+ issues. This requires LGBTI+ institutions to build political diplomacy into their activism at the national level.

Table 1: Demographic qualities of the participants

| Participants Code: ABX AB: Country X: Number | Sex | Sexual Orientation | Age | Organisation/ Location |
|---|---|---|---|---|
| TR1 | Male | Gay | 33 | Siyah Pembe Üçgen / Izmir |
| TR2 | Male | Gay | 31 | Siyah Pembe Üçgen / Izmir |
| TR3 | Female | Trans woman | 33 | Siyah Pembe Üçgen / Izmir |
| TR4 | Female | Trans woman | 21 | Siyah Pembe Üçgen / Izmir |
| TR5 | Female | Lesbian | 35 | Kaos GL/ Ankara |
| TR6 | Male | Straight | 36 | Kaos GL/ Ankara |
| TR7 | Male | Straight | 36 | Kaos GL/ Ankara |
| TR8 | Female | Trans woman | 28 | Pembe Hayat/ Ankara |
| TR9 | Female | Lesbian | 27 | Pembe Hayat/ Ankara |
| TR10 | Male | Gay | 37 | Pembe Hayat/Ankara |
| TR11 | Female | Straight | 30 | Kaos GL/ Ankara |
| TR12 | Male | Bisexual | 31 | Kaos GL/Ankara |
| TR13 | Female | Straight | 28 | Kaos GL/Ankara |
| TR14 | Female | Bisexual | 40 | Lambda/Istanbul |
| TR15 | Female | Straight | 26 | Lambda/Istanbul |
| TR16 | Female | Bisexual | 26 | Lambda/Istanbul |
| TR17 | Female | Straight | 26 | Lambda/Istanbul |
| TR18 | Female | Trans woman | 30 | SPOD/Istanbul |
| TR19 | Male | Gay | 23 | Lambda/ Istanbul |
| TR20 | Male | Gay | 20 | Siyah Pembe Üçgen/ Izmir |
| | | | | |
| UK1 | Male | Gay | 50 | GBA/ London |
| UK2 | Male | Gay | 80 | Outrage/London |
| UK3 | Female | Lesbian | 56 | UNISON/London |
| UK4 | Female | Lesbian | 32 | Kaleneodinas Trust/ London |
| UK5 | Female | Lesbian | 44 | UNISON/London |
| UK6 | Female | Trans-gender Lesbian | 55 | UNISON/London |
| UK7 | Male | Bisexual | 72 | GBA/London |
| UK8 | Male | Gay | 25 | Stonewall/ London |
| UK9 | Male | Gay | 49 | Gaywise/ London |
| UK10 | Male | Gay | 50 | Gaywise/ London |
| UK11 | Male | Gay | 25 | UNISON/London |
| UK12 | Male | Gay | 59 | UNISON/London |
| UK13 | Female | Lesbian | 45 | UNISON/London |
| UK14 | Male | Gay | 40 | Kaleeneodinas Trust/London |
| UK15 | Male | Gay | 21 | Stonewall/London |
| UK16 | Female | Lesbian | 36 | Gaywise/London |
| UK17 | Male | Gay | 47 | GBA/London |
| UK18 | Female | Lesbian | 35 | UNISON/London |
| UK19 | Male | Gay | 46 | GBA/London |
| UK20 | Male | Gay | 62 | GBA/London |

## RESEARCH METHOD

The field work of this study is qualitative as the topic is original and the study focuses on a small number of LGBTI+ institutions from which rich data is garnered (Marshall and Rossman, 2006). The empirical dimension of this research involved discourse analysis of interviews with the members of LGBTI+ organisations in Turkey and the UK. Based on the snowball sampling, in-depth semi-structured interviews were conducted with 40 members (20 in each country). Snowball sampling method was used to reach the members of LGBTI+ organisations due to the fact that the first author faced difficulties to convince members of LGBTI+ institutions for interviews at the first phase of the study. For instance, even though numerous e-mails and telephone calls were made to make appointments in Turkey, these cold calls did not generate sufficient breadth and depth of interviews. For this reason, personal networks were mobilised to contact LGBTI+ organisations. A similar procedure was followed in the UK. After the first interview that the first author conducted with a member of the organisations, every interviewee provided another person to become an interviewee for the research. The central goal of this type of snowball sampling is to reach key informants who are able to give information-rich insights in the given field (Patton, 2002).

Table 1 outlines the demographic qualities of the participants of this research and the data was transcribed and categorised through NVivo 11. The interview questions mainly focus on the aims of the LGBTI+ organisations.

## FINDINGS

In this section, we report the findings from the LGBTI+ organisations in Turkey and the UK, respectively.

## LGBTI+ ORGANISATIONS AND THEIR AIMS IN TURKEY

The findings demonstrate that the aims of the organisations in Turkey divided into six sub-sections. These are "practices against discrimination", "practices against social isolation", "events for solidarity", "advocacy", "developing the academy", and "obtaining legitimacy for LGBTI+ organisations".

### Practices against Discrimination

The main practice of LGBTI+ organisations is that of creating strategies for the purpose of overcoming discrimination against LGBTI+ individuals. The LGBTI+ organisations have a project-based approach to address discrimination issues. In order to formulate anti-discrimination strategies,

Turkish LGBTI+ organisations have to collaborate with one another and organise collaborative projects. This situation indicates that the organisations create events or projects either individually or by collaborating with other organisations in different cities. A lesbian member of Pink Life describes one such project as follows:

*We currently have two projects which are against hate crimes and discrimination and which are under the purview of the Rainbow Project. This project is composed of events such as seminars and talks and publishes some materials in order to indicate the current challenges of LGBTI+ in Turkey. Pink Life mainly focuses on trans-individuals; thus, we have also published a book with interviews with trans-women and is free of charge within the purpose of the project. We also organised a trans-women camp last year (TR Interviewee 9, Lesbian, 27, Ankara)*

The interviewee indicates the two main topics on their agenda as hate crimes and discrimination. Hate crimes are often committed against trans-women because they are the most visible and the most stigmatised among subgroups in the LGBTI+ movement. The Rainbow Project has two separate methods for overcoming issues of discrimination and creating awareness about such hate crimes throughout the country. The first method is that of organising talks and seminars at universities and public places, and the second method is that of publishing some magazines and books. Diagnosing problems related to discrimination and having voice through universities and publications have been seen an important step to increase their legitimacy in Turkey. For this reason, they focus on challenges and suggestions that provide legitimacy for them. Yet, it is important to note that these talks and publications remain limited in terms of reach and often attract other LGBTI+ individuals and allies. Wider acceptance of LGBTI+ issues in Turkey may help move the LGBTI+ speeches and publications from preaching to the converted to a much wider public audience. For this, LGBTI+ organisations need to engage with national public media, which remains a challenge in the current socio-political climate.

### Practices against Social Isolation

LGBTI+ individuals understand social isolation as being loneliness and a feeling of being separated from other individuals in the society. For this reason, practices for the purpose of counteracting the social isolation of LGBTI+ individuals have come to the agenda of these organisations. The interviews have demonstrated the organisations' difficulties with overcoming social isolation without creating LGBTI+ organisations since they are the main drivers of raising LGBTI+ awareness in society. For this reason, the organisations interpret the role of raising awareness regarding LGBTI+ issues as a responsibility to themselves. Interviewee 1 describes some of the ways in which they aim to overcome social isolation:

*We, as an organisation, care about conquering social isolation amongst LGBTI+*

*individuals. For this reason, we try to create some events with LGBTI+ friends such as meetings, watching movies together, go to places for the purpose of relaxing, having picnics, etc. (TR Interviewee 1, Gay, 33, Izmir)*

Interviewee 1 demonstrates how organisations have been trying to conquer social isolation. There exist, however, societal aspects of overcoming isolation as well. Interviewee 2 lists the practices that they have with respect to combatting isolation in society as follows:

*People, sometimes, suppose some wrong things as being right. I say this in order to indicate society's bias towards LGBTI+ individuals, who are classified as being perverts. So they adopt an exclusionist attitude towards LGBTI+ individuals. This way of treating us is the topic of the workshops which we deliver at organisations, including municipalities, parties and city councils. We create such workshops because we wish to overcome the social bias which causes social isolation for LGBTI+ individuals. (TR Interviewee 2, Gay, 31, Izmir).*

Both interviewees 1 and 2 indicate two types of practices that their organisations utilise for the purpose of combating the social isolation of LGBTI+ individuals. The first practice tries to portray LGBTI+ individuals as friends and focuses on creating social networks amongst them. The second practice includes raising society's awareness of their plight. For, even though LGBTI+ individuals collaborate and have created social networks amongst themselves, the fact still remains that they live in society and need to survive in that society as best they can in order to obtain, not only a job but health services as well. Furthermore, the LGBTI+ organisations' efforts to combat social isolation are driven by demand and voluntarism, that is the voluntary demand by individuals and organisations. In the absence of protective legislation and progressive social attitudes it is difficult for LGBTI+ organisations to deliver the message for combatting their message about dealing with social isolation to the general Turkish public. Therefore, the LGBTI+ organisations' efforts are important yet they remain partial.

### Events for Solidarity

All of the interviewees mention the significance of creating solidarity amongst LGBTI+ individuals. The reason for the drive for solidarity stems from the need to stand against the adverse social norms and practices together. Since the LGBTI+ individuals are members of sexual minorities, which face discrimination and adverse attitudes as individuals in every institution of society, they need a collective voice to progress their claims for equality. Even though the majority of people do not belong to the LGBTI+ community, LGBTI+ individuals also receive support and solidarity from non LGBTI+ allies in society. Women are more likely than men to be allies of LGBTI+, even if they are heterosexual just as a 26-year-old Straight Woman in Istanbul stated as follows:

*I am one of the volunteers in this organisation and am aware of the adverse conditions that LGBTI+ face within society. I support their rights and have some good LGBTI+ friends. Therefore, even though I am not a lesbian, I am happy to be a part of this organisation. I strongly support their obtaining their rights by attending their meetings and contributing to their events. (TR Interviewee 15, Straight Woman, 26, Istanbul)*

Solidarity changes its context with regard to the agenda of the LGBTI+ organisations because they can observe the success of their campaigns in challenging contemporary politics and social norms which are discriminatory. A 40-year-old bisexual woman explains the changing context of solidarity as follows:

*The events or campaigns of our organisation can change from time to time. For instance, we sometimes raised LGBTI+ issues by means of holding street campaigns in the past. Nevertheless, we have given great importance to their legal struggle and have conducted interviews with parliamentarians. For now, we can say that we mostly give importance to solidarity through events, cultural studies, and weekend activities such as meetings and parties. Lesbian-bisexual women meetings are one of the meetings which we hold on a monthly basis. In this way, we feel stronger. (TR Interviewee 14, Bisexual Woman, 40, Istanbul)*

LGBTI+ organisations, however, have different aims in terms of providing solidarity. As Interviewee 14 stated in their interview, the organisation's aims are primarily that of organising campaigns such as meetings and cultural activities. Nevertheless, LGBTI+ organisations can hold different aims in their various organisations. For instance, even though Pink Life (the name of an LGBTI+ organisation in Ankara) focuses on trans-women, LGB people nevertheless work for this organisation as well. In terms of solidarity, Pink Life's main aim is that of providing legal support to discriminated trans-women. Furthermore, the organisation also lobbies the parliament. This demonstrates how the concept of solidarity changes with regard to the aims of different LGBTI+ organisations. A 28-year-old Trans-woman describes the practice of solidarity in her organisation as follows:

*This is an organisation of transsexuals. The reason for establishing this organisation was for the purpose of providing solidarity amongst trans-genders. The main aims of our organisation are to write reports of acts of violence committed against transwomen and in order to support trans-genders by means of psychosocial services and legal supports; furthermore, it also aims to protect the LGBTI+ rights specifically of trans-genders by means of advocacy and to increase the visibility of trans-genders, both in society and in media. (Interviewee 8, Trans-woman, 28, Ankara)*

Interviewee 8 demonstrates the fact that LGBTI+ organisations provide various activities and supports for LGBTI+ individuals. The members of these organisations believe that those activities and supports are a source of solidarity in the LGBTI+ community. When the interviewees mentioned solidarity in relation to their own organisation's purposes, they emphasised that they feel they are in a safe environment and that they feel strong in terms of protecting LGBTI+ rights as human rights because they can also have the professional supports of both lawyers and psychologist. The findings show that solidarity provides LGBTI+ with strength by giving them both visibility and a collective voice in the adverse social and political context of the country.

## Advocacy

The interviews demonstrate that advocacy is another dimension related to the aims of LGBTI+ organisations in Turkey. The organisations use the concept in terms of the legal support provided to LGBTI+ individuals via the organisation. Based on the interviews, however, there are various contexts for advocacy. The participants of this study categorise advocacy into four different contexts: viz. transsexuals, LGBTI+ refugees, LGBs, and international advocacy. We broadly discuss each context based on the interviews. First, a 37-year-old Gay respondent describes the legal support provided to transsexuals as follows:

*Transsexual rights are crucial in contrast to LGBs because they are more visible than LGBs and, thus, it is more difficult for them to find jobs. For this reason, trans-women are often forced to work as sex workers. This situation creates violations against trans-women. For this reason, we specifically try to provide studies related to protecting the rights of trans-women. Nevertheless, we also have conducted studies for LGBs. (TR Interviewee 10, Gay, 37, Ankara)*

Interviewee 10 demonstrates the fact that their organisation specialises in guaranteeing the rights of transgenders because of the visibility and specific vulnerability of trans- women. Even though most members and volunteers of this organisation (Pink Life- Ankara) are composed of trans-women, the organisation also has LGB members. For this reason, the organisation gives importance to LGB rights as well.

The second context of advocacy regards LGBTI+ organisations which specialising in advocating for LGBTI+ refugees by providing them with legal advice and support. A 35-year-old lesbian woman describes the way she was provided with legal support by making the following comment:

*Turkey is not a country which accepts refugees, but when refugees come to the Turkey, the country gives billet, which is also called as satellite town for those refugees. When they arrive here, these refugees do not have the right to work, receive an education, or receive health rights. This makes life really bad for trans-women in those towns. It is for these reasons that we conducted studies for the purpose of protecting those trans-gender women's rights in those towns. This is based on the good-will agreement of the United Nations. (TR Interviewee 5, Lesbian, 35, Ankara)*

Other LGBTI+ organisations in Turkey focus primarily on LGBs simply because they have divided themselves into two sections — namely, Transsexuals and LGBs — in order to better provide advocacy in both national and international areas. When there is conflict amongst parties at the national level, LGBTI+ organisations protect LGBTI+ rights in international organisations, such as suing Turkey in the Court of Human Rights. On the other hand, international advocacy by LGBTI+ organisations also occurs when attending international meetings. LGBTI+ organisations are member organisations of the International Lesbian and Gay Association (ILGA); therefore, they are able to submit progress reports to this organisation. This organisation's importance comes from its bi-monthly meetings with the European Commission. Thus, LGBTI+ organisations in Turkey can raise the issues of Turkish LGBTI+ in the international arena. ILGA is an important organisation because it is recognised by the European Union. This helps LGBTI+ organisations in Turkey demand the rights of LGBTI+ in Turkey by means of the European Union. In addition, LGBTI+ organisations attend some meetings which are organised by the Ministry of European Union in Turkey. At such meetings, they can advocate the rights of LGBTI+ in Turkey. A 26-year-old Straight woman (Interviewee 17, Straight Woman, 26, Istanbul) stated that international and national advocacy could be achieved through the European Union, the Court of Human Rights, ILGA, and meetings with the Ministry of the European Union with all non-governmental organisations, including those representing LGBTI+ individuals in Turkey.

## Developing the Academy

LGBTI+ organisations aim to support academic institutions such as universities. The main Kaos GL in Ankara is an LGBTI+ organisation, which focuses on promoting academic knowledge regarding LGBTI+ in Turkey. During the interview process, most LGBTI+ organisations stressed the importance of giving seminars and talks instead of specifically focusing on academic institutions. Kaos GL, however, emphasised the role of academia in achieving LGBTI+ equality. The members of Kaos GL include many academics. Through these connections, the organisation's other members have succeeded in gaining admittance to universities as both undergraduates and masters students. A 35-year-old lesbian member of Kaos GL describes this process as follows:

*We aim to develop academia in terms of their knowledge about Sexual Minorities. For this reason, we have an academic committee which is composed of thirty to forty individuals. The professors and doctors at these universities have attended meetings in order to describe the next year's goals in terms of LGBTI+ studies. We also provide a master programme at Ankara University which is related to criticising heterosexist thoughts. We also give talks for some courses at Hacettepe Univerity, Ankara University, and Baskent University. As our next goal, we aim to create an introduction to homosexuality which covers a range of topics regarding sexual orientation, as well as several definitions of gender identity. Actually, academics in the Department of Psychology and Psychological Counselling at some universities have tried to open such a course. (TR Interview 5, Lesbian, 35, Ankara)*

The development of academic knowledge is, thus, a very important step for LGBTI+ organisations in terms of creating a positive understanding towards sexual minorities in education. This process indicates that the LGBTI+ movement has the support of some academics in universities, because when universities provide LGBTI+ organisations with the opportunity to give lectures or seminars at their institutions, it brings legitimacy to the LGBTI+ organisations. We discuss this in detail, however, in the following section

## Obtaining Legitimacy for LGBTI+ Organisations

Legitimacy is an important indicator for LGBTI+ organisations to be more effective in achieving their aims. Having a legal status could protect LGBTI+ organisations against unfair treatment. During the LGBTI+ movement in Turkey, LGBTI+ organisations faced many challenges from other governmental institutions. For this reason, LGBTI+ organisations have aimed at achieving legitimacy by gaining the support of different institutions which do not, themselves, specifically focus on LGBTI+ issues. The LGBTI+ movement started with a few people trying to provide networks for LGBTI+ individuals in Turkey in the 1990s. These organisations, however, only gained legal status in 2005. Before 2005, even though there were a number of LGBTI+ organisations in Turkey, they were considered simply as initiatives rather than non-governmental organisations. For this reason, gaining the legal status of "non-governmental organisation" was an important step for legitimacy because, as Lewis (2009: 4) points out, 'NGOs can oppose, complement or reform the state but they cannot ignore it.' In addition to their gaining a legal status from the state, LGBTI+ organisations in Turkey became members of ILGA-Europe. As a 33-year-old transwoman stated:

*Our organisation gained the legal status of NGO by becoming a member of ILGA which is a well-known organisation throughout the world. This allows us to raise awareness about our problems in the international arena. (TR Interviewee 3, Trans-woman, 33, Izmir)*

ILGA-Europe is an important organisation recognised for fighting for the global LGBTI+ movement. LGBTI+ organisations across Europe, including Turkey, have joined this organisation in order to raise awareness about their national LGBTI+ issues to the international arena. For this reason, the organisations in Turkey are members of ILGA-Europe. Apart from obtaining legitimacy by means of gaining legal status and becoming a member of ILGA, the LGBTI+ organisations aim at gaining societal legitimacy as well. In order to do that, the members of the organisations give talks to the municipalities, which invite them to inform their local citizens about LGBTI+ issues. On the other hand, the organisations also give lectures at universities and support academicians. All of these practices are sources of legitimacy for LGBTI+ organisations. A 37-year-old gay respondent states the reason that NGO LGBTI+ organisations do this as follows:

> *The decision of LGBTI+ initiatives to become NGOs in order to provide LGBTI+s visibility in public areas and in order to be able to demand LGBTI+ rights from the state. This had given us the opportunity to include universities and municipalities in our movement because, when we gained legitimacy, it demonstrated that we are not illegal organisations. (TR Interviewee 10, Gay, 37, Ankara)*

In addition to the sources of legitimacy mentioned above, some members of LGBTI+ organisations think that the Gezi Park Protests also provided legitimacy for both the LGBTI+ movement and its organisations. A 35-year-old lesbian participant (Interviewee 5) pointed out that the legitimacy gained in Gezi Park helped people who do not support the LGBTI+ movement to see that they can live together and collaborate with LGBTI+ individuals towards common goals. Thus, the Gezi Park Protests, as the largest social protest movement in the near Turkish history, contributed to the LGBTI+ movement and the legitimation of the LGBTI+ organisations.

On the other hand, LGBTI+ organisations also faced legitimacy challenges. The documentary reviews of the reports and studies of LGBTI+ organisations in Turkey (Kaos GL, 2014) revealed that the LGBTI+ organisations experienced significant challenges to their organisational freedom to serve and organisational survival due to limited nature of the legitimacy that they were afforded.

The first challenge is to achieve organisational freedom, which is about the challenges in pursuit of acquiring full set of rights for establishing LGBTI+ organisations as associations. In Turkey, there is no need to obtain permission from state bodies in order to establish an association (5253 Associations Law, 2004). At first glance, there appears to be broad freedom for individuals who create associations; nevertheless, there are some limitations. An association cannot violate public morality and family values, and the Turkish constitution does not have equality based on sexual orientation and sexual identity (Constitution of Turkey, 1982). As stated in the discriminative approach taken by politicians, the recognition of state officers affects the legitimacy of LGBTI+ organisations. Even though the state gives freedom to establish associations, this is a generic provision which the LGBTI+ groups try to utilise. Yet the state tries to limit institutional rights of the LGBTI+ organisations as NGOs under the guise of protection of the values of society. The challenge of the state creates difficulties for LGBTI+ organisation in Turkey. In order to have a better environment for

24

organisational freedom, LGBTI+ organisations publish reports on how regulations can be changed to improve conditions for LGBTI+ organisations (International Gay and Lesbian Human Rights Commission, 2014).

The second challenge is the challenge of organisational survival. Even though LGBTI+ organisations have been around for over a decade now, they face problems in relation to the biased interpretation of laws. For instance, Van Governorate sued the *Genclik ve Ekoloji Dernegi* (the *Youth and Ecology Association*) for their studies on sexual orientation. The governorate claimed that the practices of the organisation were against the Turkish Civil Code, which states that associations cannot have any goals which are against the law and which traduce public morality. In the end, the association won the lawsuit against the governorate. This case presents prime example of the challenges to survival of LGBTI+ organisations.

Although the LGBTI+ organisations have gained a degree of legitimacy in Turkey, the extent to which they can realise their legitimacy as freedom is severely constrained. The challenges to the freedom of association and even the longevity of LGBTI+ organisations renders their activities more challenging in Turkey in comparison to their counterparts in other European countries.

## LGBTI+ ORGANISATIONS AND THEIR AIMS IN THE UK

The findings demonstrate that the aims of the organisations in the UK divided into three sub-sections. These are "the welfare of LGBTI+ Community", "Raising awareness about LGBTI+ issues", and "organising events regarding LGBTI+".

### The Welfare of LGBTI+ Community

The LGBTI+ organisations in the UK have aimed at making the life conditions and careers of LGBTI+ individuals in the UK better. In order to achieve these goals, they work for the protection of LGBTI+ rights and support LGBTI+ by means of projects and training programmes which are able to provide them with career opportunities. A 25 year-old gay member of Stonewall describes the programmes as follows:

*We proceed with the personal development program [sic.] to ensure that we offer training for future LGBTI+ leaders and also to make sure that we promote their right to work. (UK Interviewee 8, gay, 25, London)*

In addition to creating training and personal development (PD) programmes for LGBTI+ individuals, the organisations focus on persuading those who make decisions, politicians, and cabinet ministers for the purpose of gaining more rights. For instance, the right for gay people to marry is a recent achievement of the LGBTI+ organisations. They understand the process of gaining rights as being 'one step at the time [across the] organisational networks amongst the organisations.' One of the participants of this research (Interviewee 2, Gay, 80, London) points out the need for organisational networks by giving the example of Stonewall's collaborations with other LGBTI+ organisations.

Whilst LGBTI+ organisations aim at protecting LGBTI+ rights by providing them with support for their careers; they also consider the minorities within the LGBTI+ community. There are calls for an intersectional approach (Tatli and Ozbilgin 2012, Ozbilgin et al 2011) to diversity as well as LGBTI+ issues in the UK. A 49-year-old gay man describes this situation as follows:

> *We are interested in the issues of [the] LGBTI+ community [by] considering issues of ethnic minorities within LGBTI+ community such as [the] Black Asian minority. It is important to be aware of ethnic minorities among LGBTI+ because discrimination is not only based on being LGBTI+. Sometimes, both being LGBTI+ and belonging [to a] minority group have created discrimination. For this reason, we also aim at protecting LGBTI+ rights [by] considering ethnic minorities. (UK Interviewee 9, Gay, 49, London)*

This participant indicates the importance of ethnic minorities within LGBTI+ groups. Even though he raised this issue, other LGBTI+ organisations have raised the same issue as well in describing the nature of discrimination. The organisations also provide legal consultancy for ethnic minorities in LGBTI+ groups.

## Raising Awareness about LGBTI+ Issues

LGBTI+ organisations also focus on raising issues regarding health, such as HIV and AIDS and creating an international agenda for LGBTI+. In this section, we will firstly state how the organisations provide awareness regarding health issues and then will point out how LGBTI+ organisations aim to create an international agenda.

LGBTI+ organisations have projects which are funded by both international and national agencies. A 50-year-old gay man gives an example of a project regarding the awareness of health issues in sexual relationships of gay men as follows:

> *We did a project on the sexual needs of gay men [by] considering issues of HIV in the sexual relationship[s]. What we have done was to look at informal interviews of a range of gay men that we were targeting. We profiled some of the issues and the concerns that they have and the scenarios they found themselves engaging in sexual activities which may pose a risk to them, and we created a series of workshops to develop a drama piece that explored the issue of [protecting one's self from] HIV [and] unprotected sex.*

*(UK Interviewee 10, Gay, 50, London)*

As the participant stated, LGBTI+ organisations organise workshops and work on LGBTI+-related projects. The organisations have made a crucial contribution to LGBTI+ individuals in society by conducting research, workshops, and training programmes for them. On the other hand, these organisations have raised issues about other countries' organisations and LGBTI+ individuals throughout Europe. LGBTI+ organisations (especially Stonewall) in the UK have also played leading roles in the international arena. In this way, they hope to raise the rights of LGBTI+ individuals internationally. As a 32-year-old lesbian participant states:

*[w]e are an organisation that concentrates exclusively on LGBTI+ rights internationally. International media often approaches us to get comments regarding LGBTI+ issues, and we raise awareness through both media and members of parliament (MPs). For instance, when [an] MP [of the UK] visited Cameroon and Kenya, we were able to give [them] country briefings regarding LGBTI+ rights and local activists. (UK Interviewee 4, Lesbian, 32, London)*

The main reason for providing awareness about LGBTI+ issues comes from the need to protect LGBTI+ individuals against any strand of discrimination and for the purpose of trying to provide both legal rights and equal opportunities for LGBTI+ both in their social life and for their careers. As we state in this section, LGBTI+ organisations have also created workshops and training programmes related to LGBTI+ issues.

In the next section, we explain what kinds of event the LGBTI+ organisations organise for the purpose of protecting LGBTI+ rights, promoting the welfare of LGBTI+, and raising LGBTI+ issues at both the national and international levels. These events make a contribution to increasing the legitimacy of LGBTI+ in the UK; because the events make LGBTI+ organisations more visible, and they provide access to many people.

## Organising Events regarding LGBTI+s

In this section, we discuss the events that LGBTI+ organisations hold. These mainly include national conferences and purposive meetings. National conferences are one of the events that LGBTI+ organisations organise. For instance, Unison hosts a range of national conferences, with the organisation having a national LGBTI+ committee composed of 38 members. Unison also has 12 regional groups for LGBTI+ members. This makes it easy and relatively effective for these organisations to create national conferences. The conferences mostly cover themes around LGBTI+ rights, LGBTI+ issues, and discrimination.

Purposive meetings are the other type of event which the LGBTI+ organisations utilise. There are two reasons for holding purposive meetings.

The first is saving time. Because the members of these organisations believe that a large number of people at a meeting without any purpose cannot efficiently listen and talk. UK Interviewee 2 states that this type of meeting tends to exclude people who either do not have the time or do not have the inclination to spend an evening talking and listening to other fellow members. For this reason, his organisation organises particular events in particular places. People who believe that the meeting relates to them can attend the meeting, thereby it saves the members time. The second reason for holding purposive meetings is that of strengthening the capacity of LGBTI+ activists by improving their skills, as a 47-year-old gay man states:

> [w]e organise lecture series, and we invite international activists to the series from many countries, such as Poland and Jamaica, to talk regarding the challenges that they face in their countries. Thus, we can both raise the international awareness of LGBTI+ issues and create purposive meetings in order to save time. Otherwise, general meetings do not [achieve] time efficiency. For this reason, we always define an important purpose [in order] to make it real. (UK Interviewee 17, Gay, 47, London)

This interview shows that purposive meetings are for optimising the time spent for its members and creating a significant capacity among members to achieve a high impact on the country at large.

## DISCUSSION AND CONCLUSION

Drawing on in-depth interviews with 149 LGBTI+ employees within 14 case study organisations in the UK, Colgan and McKearney (2012) explain that LGBTI+ organisations play an important role in terms of creating visibility and increasing the voice of LGBTI+ individuals in society. LGBTI+ organisations play a similar role in Turkey. Through their engagement with national and international level stakeholders and public, the LGBTI+ organisations in Turkey seek to raise awareness, despite contextual constraints that prevent them from realising their full potential to affect changes and impact policy and practices. Nevertheless, the two countries have different environments for LGBTI+. Both LGBTI+ individuals and LGBTI+ organisations have gained wider legal and social legitimacy in recent years; Turkey, on the other hand, only provides unintentional legitimacy for its LGBTI+ organisations, which benefit from the legitimacy offered by the general right to establish NGOs (Ozeren and Aydin, 2016; Aydin, 2017). LGBTI+ individuals however remain widely exposed to discrimination and unfavourable treatment across all aspects of their lives. Due to the divergent roots that the LGBTI+ activism and organising have taken in both countries, the LGBTI+ organisations in both countries have different priorities, aims and strategies in their own contexts. Whilst the UK's LGBTI+ organisations mostly consider the welfare of the LGBTI+ community and raise awareness about LGBTI+ issues, including health issues (e.g. HIV and AIDS), the LGBTI+ organisations in Turkey aims at overcoming discrimination in the human rights context rather than simply raising awareness about LGBTI+ rights since the country does not have regulations and laws for LGBTI+. The LGBTI+ organisations in both countries have different forms of engagement with the international context. In the case of UK, the LGBTI+ organisations seek to engage with international context both to draw inspiration and to impact practice in other countries in solidarity with LGBTI+ organisations elsewhere. Whereas in the case of Turkey, LGBTI+ organisations draw legitimacy from the international context, mobilising the recognition that international organisations have in order to secure their national level legitimacy. The Turkish LGBTI+ organisation struggle with survival in the context of an increasingly antagonistic national system.

The role of the state, as a third party, is that of regulating social actors like a rule-maker, -enforcer and referee (Skocpol, 1985). Institutional theory, for this reason, emphasises the regulative pillar (i.e. demonstrating the role of laws and rules in the social order) (Yiu and Makino, 2002). Individuals, in turn, accommodate regulations because they aim, not only to gain rewards for conforming to regulations but also to avoid sanctions (Scott, 2013). The LGBTI+ organisations in Turkey cannot report much progress towards gaining recognition and legitimacy in the eyes of the state beyond the NGO status which is a generic provision that is not specific to the LGBTI+ organisations. The situation of the Turkish LGBTI+ organisations stands in contrast to what the regulative pillar of institutional theory suggests. Despite progress towards institutionalisation of LGBTI+ organising, there is still much resistance in acceptance of the legitimacy gains.

LGBTI+ organisations in Turkey have only received their legitimacy circumstantially through the laws which govern NGOs in Turkey. UK LGBTI+ organisations, on the contrary, have, gained their legitimacy from the social order. It is important to note that different struggles through legitimacy of LGBTI+ organisations in Turkey and the UK illustrates that at the nexus of social mores, social norms, significant national institutions and international players, each country presents a different and dissimilar route for LGBTI+ organisations to combat discrimination and fight for equal rights for LGBTI+ individuals. Whilst UK LGBTI+ organisations focus on the challenges which individuals might face in both the public and private sectors and provide advocacy services LGBTI+, LGBTI+ organisations in Turkey focus on gaining rights for LGBTI+ from the government because, even though they might try to advocate LGBTI+ issues in society, it is limited to simply raising awareness about these problems without having the ability to posit any substantial solutions.

The national context in Turkey proves challenging for LGBTI+ movement and organisations to gain further legitimacy (Ozbilgin 2017). Given the current situation, the Turkish Minister of Justice, Bekir Bozdag, has stated that the ruling party (i.e. the *AKP*) will not give Sexual Minorities any legal rights whatsoever. Thus, we conclude with one final yet very significant findings that the assumption of progress towards legitimacy for the LGBTI+ organisations needs to be revised as the national context can present challenges that may lead to retrenchment and back steps on the way to legitimacy. If we observe the history of criminalisation, decriminalisation, recriminalisation, legitimation and delegitimation of LGBTI+ rights in different countries, we see a very patchy path towards equal rights. Although the path to equality remains long and arduous, and sometimes with setbacks, we demonstrated in this chapter that in two distinctly different countries LGBTI+ organisations, while working with different aims, achieve more than what individual activists could muster, Solidarity and collaboration at institutional, national and international levels help LGBTI+ organisations to foster collective voice (Bell et al. 2011) pay dividends on the way to legitimate LGBTI+ organisations and to secure equal rights for LGBTI+ individuals.

## REFERENCES

Amnesty International (2011) *Not an Illness nor a Crime*. Available at: https://www.amnestyusa.org/sites/default/files/notillnessnorcrime.pdf (Accessed: 25.10. 2015).

Aydin, E. (2017) "Problems and suggestions: Non-governmental organizations of sexual orientation minorities in the context of Turkey and the UK", in Vojko Potocan, Mustafa Ungan and Zlatko Nedelko (eds), *Handbook of Research on Managerial Solutions in Non-Profit Organizations*. Hershey, PA: IGI Global, pp. 232-252.

Bell, M. P., Özbilgin, M. F., Beauregard, T. A., & Sürgevil, O. (2011) "Voice, silence, and diversity in 21st century organizations: Strategies for inclusion of gay, lesbian, bisexual, and transgender employees". *Human Resource Management*, 50(1), 131-146.

Bowring, M. A. & Brewis, J. (2009) "Truth and consequences: managing lesbian and gay identity in the Canadian workplace*", Equal Opportunities International*, 28(5), 361-377.

Colgan, F. & McKearney, A. (2012) "Visibility and voice in organisations: Lesbian, gay, bisexual and transgendered employee networks", *Equality, Diversity and Inclusion: An International Journal*, 31(4), 359-378.

Colgan, F. & Wright, T. (2011) "Lesbian, Gay and Bisexual Equality in a Modernizing Public Sector 1997-2010: Opportunities and Threats", *Gender Work and Organization*, 18(5), 548-570.

Colgan, F., Creegan, C., McKearney, A. & Wright, T. (2007) "Equality and diversity policies and practices at work: lesbian, gay and bisexual workers", *Equal Opportunities International*, 26(6), 590-609.

Duman, T., Yavuz, N. & Karakaya, N. (2016) "İnsan hakları ve demokrasi vatandaşlık bilgisi", Pegem Atıf İndeksi, 2016(3), 1-184.

Gelfand, M.J., Raver, J.L., Nishii, L., Leslie, L.M., Lun, J., Lim, B.C., Duan, L., Almaliach, A., Ang, S., Arnadottir, J., Aycan, Z., Boehnke, K., Boski, P., Cabecinhas, R., Chan, D., Chhokar, J., D'Amato, A., Ferrer, M., Fischlmayr, I.C., Fischer, R., Fulop, M., Georgas, J., Kashima, E.S., Kashima, Y., Kim, K., Lempereur, A., Marquez, P., Othman, R., Overlaet, B., Panagiotopoulou, P., Peltzer, K., Perez-Florizno, L.R., Ponomarenko, L., Realo, A., Schei, V., Schmitt, M., Smith, P.B., Soomro, N., Szabo, E., Taveesin, N., Toyama, M., Van de Vliert, E., Vohra, N., Ward, C. & Yamaguchi, S. (2011) "Differences between tight and loose cultures: a 33-nation study", *Science* (New York, N.Y.), 332(6033), 1100- 1104.

Goffman, E. (1963) *Stigma*. Englewood Cliffs: NJ: Prentice-Hall.

Kaos GL (2014) *Yogyakarta İlkeleri Işığında Türkiye'de Mevzuat ve Ayrımcılık*. Available at:

http://www.kaosgldernegi.org/resim/yayin/dl/de_mevzuat_ve_ayrimcilik.pdf (Accessed: 10.07.2015).

Kersley, B., Alpin, C., Forth, J., Bryson, A., Bewley, H., Dix, G. & Oxenbridge, S. (2013) *Inside the workplace: findings from the 2004 Workplace Employment Relations Survey*. London: Routledge.

Lewis, D. (2009) "Nongovernmental organizations, definition and history", in Anheier, H. K. and Toepler, S. (eds) *International Encyclopedia of Civil Society*. US: Springer, pp. 1056-1062.

Marshall, C. & Rossman, G.B. (2011) *Designing qualitative research*. London: Sage.

McPhail, R., McNulty, Y. & Hutchings, K. (2016) "Lesbian and gay expatriation: Opportunities, barriers and challenges for global mobility", *The International Journal of Human Resource Management*, 27(3), 382-406.

Öner, A. (2015) *Çalışma Hayatında Toplumsal Cinsiyet ve Ayrımcılık: Beyaz Yakalı Eşcinseller*. Istanbul: Iletisim.

Ozeren, E. & Aydin, E. (2016) "What Does Being LGBT Mean in the Workplace? A Comparison of LGBT Equality in Turkey and the UK", in Klarsfeld, A., Ng, E.S., Booysen, L.A.E., Christiansen, L.C. and Kuvaas, B. (eds.) *Research Handbook of International and Comparative Perspectives on Diversity Management. 1st edn*. UK: Edward Elgar.

Özbilgin, M. F. (2017) "Cinsellik ve Emek: Butler ve Bourdieu ile kazanımların kırılganlığını ve direnişi sorgulamak", *KAOSQ+*, 5: 97-106.

Özbilgin, M. F., Beauregard, T. A., Tatli, A., & Bell, M. P. (2011) "Work–life, diversity and intersectionality: a critical review and research agenda". *International Journal of Management Reviews*, 13(2), 177-198.

Öztürk, M. B. (2011) "Sexual orientation discrimination: Exploring the experiences of lesbian, gay and bisexual employees in Turkey", *Human Relations*, 64(8), 1099-1118.

Öztürk, M. B. & Özbilgin, M. (2015) "From Cradle to Grave", in Colgan, F. and Rumens, N. (eds.) *Sexual Orientation at Work: Contemporary Issues and Perspectives*. London: Routledge, pp. 152-165.

Özbek, Ç. (2017) "Ayrımcılıkla Mücadelenin Kamusallığı: LGBT, Hareket ve Örgütlülük". *Toplum ve Demokrasi Dergisi*, 11(24), 141-165.

Patton, M. Q. (2002) *Qualitative research*. London: Wiley Online Library.

Rumens, N. (2016) "Towards Queering the Business School: A Research Agenda for Advancing Lesbian, Gay, Bisexual and Trans Perspectives and Issues", *Gender, Work & Organization*, 23(1), 36-51.

Rumens, N. & Broomfield, J. (2012) "Gay men in the police: Identity disclosure and management issues", *Human Resource Management Journal*, 22(3), 283-298.

Rumens, N. & Broomfield, J. (2014) "Gay men in the performing arts: Performing sexualities within 'gay-friendly'work contexts", *Organization*, 21(3), 365- 382.

Scott, W. R. (2013) *Institutions and organizations: Ideas, interests, and identities*. London: Sage Publications.

Skocpol, T. (2013) "Bringing the state back in", in Hill, M. (ed.) The Policy Process- A Reader. 2nd edn. London: Routledge, pp. 126-138.

Tatli, A., & Özbilgin, M. F. (2012) "An emic approach to intersectional study of diversity at work: a Bourdieuan framing". *International Journal of Management Reviews*, 14(2), 180-200.

Tahaoglu, C. (2015) "Ayrımcılığın Yasal Dayanakları ve Eşcinsel Memurlar", *Çalışma Hayatında*, 1, 97-108.

Tatli, A. (2011) "A multi-layered exploration of the diversity management field: diversity discourses, practices and practitioners in the UK", *British Journal of Management*, 22(2), 238-253.

Weeks, J. (1995) *Invented moralities: Sexual values in an age of uncertainty*. London: Routledge.

Wright, T. (2015) "Women's Experience of Workplace Interactions in Male-Dominated Work: The Intersections of Gender, Sexuality and Occupational Group", *Gender, Work & Organization*, 23(3), 348-362.

Yılmaz, V. & Göçmen, I. (2016) "Denied Citizens of Turkey: Experiences of Discrimination Among LGBT Individuals in Employment, Housing and Health Care", *Gender, Work*

*& Organization*, 23 (5), 1-19.

Yiu, D. & Makino, S. (2002) "The choice between joint venture and wholly owned subsidiary: An institutional perspective", *Organization science*, 13(6), 667- 683.

Yurtsever, G. & Erdoğan, H. H. (2010) "Sexual Orientation Topics in Business Education in Turkey", *International Journal of Diversity in Organisations, Communities & Nations*, 10(2), 341- 352.

# CHAPTER 2

# A COMPARATIVE LOOK AT LGBT RIGHTS AND ACQUISITIONS: EUROPEAN UNION AND TURKEY

Gaye Gökalp Yılmaz

Same sex relationships have been an issue of debate through years beginning from ancient Rome and Greece. Especially homosexuality has been visible part of historical struggle of LGBT movement. On the other hand, masculinity have always been an issue of power and therefore, decisions based on masculinity and heteronormative codes have been neglecting and sometimes criminalizing same sex relationships in history of Europe. Religious authorities were also other actors in criminalizing homosexual relationships and religion have been a matter of issue while considering same sex acts. Within that framework, history of Europe, was not an era of liberation for homosexuals or lesbians until recent decades. However, it must be highlighted here that criminalizing and punishing LGBT people of the time were common in many historical empires of Europe. Moreover, France have decriminalized homosexuality during Napoleon era and Netherlands have favored more tolerating laws of French administration. However, Germany after its retarded unification, have been harshly punishing homosexual acts under Prussian empire (Kollman and Waites, 2009:2).

Movements for progressive sex reform that focus on same sex behavior and dissidence from gender norms have existed since at least the late nineteenth century and Magnus Hirschfeld founded the Scientific Humanitarian Committee in 1897 and later the World League for Sexual Reform, both of which campaigned against harsh punishment of same-sex sexual behavior (Kollman and Waites, 2009:3). As Kollman and Waites also quote from Adam and Waaldijk ; these movements were destroyed by the rise of fascism in Germany in the 1930s and after World War II, social organizations for homosexuals in Western societies such as Norway, Sweden and France began to reappear in the late 1940s and homosexuals in many of these continental Western European Countries enjoyed some minimal forms of citizenship as same-sex sexual activity had been de-criminalized in the Nordic countries, France, Belgium, The Netherlands, Luxembourg, Italy and Greece by the early 1950s. (Adam, 1987 and Waaldijk 2000).

While taking into consideration of LGBT people and LGBT politics in European history, it is not possible to mention a single line that explains a single historical timeline. Each country and the European Union legal history have their own significant points to highlight. These significant points cover the establishment of European Unions' values on human dignity, human rights, equality, respect for human rights and combat against discrimination on the EU law making process and Turkey's domestic law which has never criminalized and always tolerated same sex acts but has also never enacted domestic laws to protect LGBT rights specifically. This chapter intends to analyze European Unions' main values and articles providing a progress for LGBT rights and Turkey's dilemmas in "*tolerating but not protecting*" approach.

## EUROPEAN UNION'S BRIEF HISTORY ON LGBT RIGHTS AND ACQUISITIONS

The issue of same sex behavior and homosexuality have evolved from "being de-criminalizing act" or omitting the codes criminalizing same sex acts as "illegal" to an issue of "human rights" through European Union establishments. This was a broad change in understanding of the issue as a "*human right*" and preventing discrimination against LGBT people and adjusting the laws and regulations of European Union and member states. The issue of the rights of gays and lesbians appeared on the EU stage in the early 1980s when the European Parliament, after heated discussion, adopted the Sqarcialupi Report (European Parliament 1984). In this report, the European Commission was asked to table proposals to combat discrimination against homosexuals in employment (Swiebel, 2009: 22). Following Sqarcialupi Report, 1990s have brought more efforts for LGBT rights and fighting against discrimination towards LGBT people have become a significant agenda for European Union.

Swiebel briefly mention the historical process of LGBT rights and acquisitions in European Union and member states, at the beginning of 1990s, as follows;

*In 1993, the European Commission-funded book, edited by Clapham and Waaldijk (1993), was published with its telltale title: Homosexuality – a European Community Issue. Initially, national differences in the treatment of homosexuals were considered an internal market issue; the argument was that such differences would be an obstacle to the free movement of persons within the Community. Later, the increased focus on social issues offered a convenient stepping stone for the rights of gays and lesbians. In the Medium-Term Social Action Programme 1995 – 7, the European Commission proclaimed its interest in social policy and stressed the role played by the dialogue between member states, employers, trade unions and civil partners (Hantrais 2007, p.*

*14). Promptly, the newly founded and Commission-funded European branch of the International Lesbian and Gay Association (ILGA)-Europe, presented 'equality for lesbians and gay men' as a relevant issue in the 'civil and social dialogue' (Beger et al.1998). In this way, in the early 1990s, the LGBT movement gained access to at least two EU institutions, the European Parliament and the European Commission (Swiebel, 2009: 22).*

European Parliament continued to work on the agenda of LGBT rights and with International Gay and Lesbian Association (ILGA) and single states' politicians, like Claudia Roth of Germany, have started to deal with the issue of combatting with discrimination and providing rights for marriage and adoption of children and make discussions available on a broader political area and public domain.

*In 1994, the European Parliament adopted a second report on gay and lesbian rights with considerable input from ILGA-Europe. This report, by the German Green MP Claudia Roth, asked for measures to combat discrimination against gays and lesbians in all spheres of life and even put the issues of marriage and adoption on the table (European Parliament 1994). The Roth Report raised the profile of gay and lesbian's rights, and this influenced the then upcoming treaty reform negotiations. The issue was for the first time 'mainstreamed' into general political debates. In 1996, the European Parliament asked for the inclusion in the new treaty of 'the principle of equal treatment and non-discrimination regardless, in particular, of race, gender, sexual orientation, age, religion or handicap' (European Parliament 1996). This clause was the result of the lobbying efforts to add a specific competence to combat racial discrimination and – partly as a bandwagon effect – to combat discrimination on other grounds to the treaties. The ground of 'sexual orientation' was the most controversial of this list. The final result was the now famous Article 13 of the EC Treaty (TEC), adopted by the 1997 Amsterdam European Council, that enlarged the EU's competence to take measures against discrimination that went beyond the labour market and included five new discrimination grounds – among them sexual orientation. This happy result was finally settled in 1997 at the Summit of Amsterdam. (Swiebel, 2009: 22).*

Following Treaty of Amsterdam 1997, Treaty on European Union (TEU) enacted in 2008, included article 2 and article 3 that created legal basis for principle of equality and prohibition of discrimination on the basis of sexual orientation.

Article 2 [1]

*The Union is founded on the values of respect for human dignity, freedom, democracy, equality, the rule of law and respect for human rights, including the rights of persons belonging to minorities. These values are common to the Member States in a society in which pluralism, non-discrimination, tolerance, justice, solidarity and equality between women and men prevail.*

---

[1] https://eur-lex.europa.eu/LexUriServ/LexUriServ.do?uri=OJ:C:2008:115:0013:0045:EN:PDF

This article of TEU mainly puts basic humanitarian values of EU to the forefront and emphasize human dignity, equality, freedom, respect for human rights and rights of minorities. People with different sexual orientations should be treated equally without any consideration of difference. Moreover, member states should be subject to this treaty and this article by taking into account concepts of "pluralism" grasping all kinds of differences, "non-discrimination", equal treatment for all people, "tolerance" for differences and embracing the dignity of differences in a community and also gender equality between women and men.

Article 3 (ex Article 2 of TEU)

*1.    The Union's aim is to promote peace, its values and the well-being of its peoples.*

*2.    The Union shall offer its citizens an area of freedom, security and justice without internal frontiers, in which the free movement of persons is ensured in conjunction with appropriate measures with respect to external border controls, asylum, immigration and the prevention and combating of crime.*

*3.    The Union shall establish an internal market. It shall work for the sustainable development of Europe based on balanced economic growth and price stability, a highly competitive social market economy, aiming at full employment and social progress, and a high level of protection and improvement of the quality of the environment. It shall promote scientific and technological advance.*

*It shall combat social exclusion and discrimination, and shall promote social justice and protection, equality between women and men, solidarity between generations and protection of the rights of the child.*

*It shall promote economic, social and territorial cohesion, and solidarity among Member States.*

*It shall respect its rich cultural and linguistic diversity, and shall ensure that Europe's cultural heritage is safeguarded and enhanced.*

*4.    The Union shall establish an economic and monetary union whose currency is the euro.*

*5.    In its relations with the wider world, the Union shall uphold and promote its values and interests and contribute to the protection of its citizens. It shall contribute to peace, security, the sustainable development of the Earth, solidarity and mutual respect among peoples, free and fair trade, eradication of poverty and the protection of human rights, in particular the rights of the child, as well as to the strict observance and the development of international law, including respect for the principles of the United Nations Charter.*

*6.    The Union shall pursue its objectives by appropriate means commensurate with the competences which are conferred upon it in the Treaties.*

Article 3 with its subtitles, covers a broad range of issues regarding social and economic life. 1st subtitle of article 3, emphasize the significance of values of the EU based on peace and well-being of the people. This emphasis on well-being and peace is empowered with 2nd subtitles first sentence that mentions *The Union shall offer its citizens an area of freedom* and puts freedom as one of the most significant value of the Union and dignity that citizens should be provided.

In 3rd subtitle of the TEU article 3, the basic consideration seems on establishment of an Internal Market of the Union and a competitive market economy with intentions of the full employment and progress and in addition this subtitle ends with a statement that highlights an atmosphere of equality and inclusion; *It shall combat social exclusion and discrimination, and shall promote social justice and protection, equality between women and men, solidarity between generations and protection of the rights of the child.* Moreover, although some statements of article 3 seem to be related with economy and economic regulations, article display a comprehension of the Union that economy and social cohesion are equally significant. Thus, economic activities and regulations in the market are considered as matters of human rights, equality and social and economic inclusion. Inclusion appears as a value that should be established through combatting against discrimination. Therefore, equality brings tolerance, social and economic inclusion to the forefront and discrimination is seen as a violation of basic human rights. Additionally, 5th subtitle of article 3, states that *It shall contribute to peace, security, the sustainable development of the Earth, solidarity and mutual respect among peoples, free and fair trade, eradication of poverty and the protection of human rights…* and this statement emphasize main values of the Union peace, respect and security of the Earth and people living on it.

After TEU issued in 2008, another Treaty regulating functioning of European Union (TFEU) has been enacted. Treaty on Functioning of the European Union (TFEU) has come into effect in 2012 and prohibited discrimination on grounds of sexual orientation in European Union primary law in art. $10^2$*In defining and implementing its policies and activities, the Union shall aim to combat discrimination based on sex, racial or ethnic origin, religion or belief, disability, age or sexual orientation.*

Article 19 (ex Article 13 TEC)[3]

*1. Without prejudice to the other provisions of the Treaties and within the limits of the powers conferred by them upon the Union, the Council, acting unanimously in accordance with a special legislative procedure and after obtaining the consent of the European Parliament, may take appropriate action to combat discrimination based on sex, racial or ethnic origin, religion or*

---

[2] https://europadatenbank.iaaeu.de/user/view_legalact.php?id=254
[3] https://eur-lex.europa.eu/resource.html?uri=cellar:2bf140bf-a3f8-4ab2-b506 fd71826e6da6.0023. 02/DOC_2&format=PDF

*belief, disability, age or sexual orientation.*

Article 19 of TFEU, empowered the EU to adopt measures to deal with discrimination based on other grounds including sexual orientation. With that article the significant consideration of discrimination against sexual orientation is put into the agenda as serious as racial, ethnic or religious origin.

After narrating into legal basis and provisions of European Union on sexual orientation and combat against discrimination, it is possible to highlight that these articles of TFEU and TEU intends to establish a LGBT friendly community and legal framework among its member states. On the global spectrum, EU appears comparatively LGBT friendly and EU member states are parties to a whole range of international instruments including European Convention of Human Rights (ECHR) which set out a catalogue of fundamental rights for all. (Shreeves, 2018: 2). In addition, Shreeves presents that at the same time, the EU boasts one of the most extensive sets of anti-discrimination legislation in the world and moreover, the EU promotes the rights of LGBTI people internationally. Amongst numerous examples, it initiated a UN declaration calling for the worldwide decriminalisation of homosexuality (Shreeves, 2012:2) As Shreeves display a broad outlook regarding LGBTI rights all over the world and state that negative perceptions of LGBTI people are reflected in harsh laws and consensual same sex acts between adults are illegal at least 72 countries and in eight of these (Iran, Saudi Arabia, Yemen, regions of Somalia, Nigeria and Iraq and ISIL/Da'esh- held territories of Syria, whilst in a further five (Afghanistan, Mauritania, Pakistan, Qatar, UAE it remains technically possible but lesser penalties are being invoked), they are punishable by death (Shreeves, 2018: 2).

## LGBT PROVISIONS IN TURKEY A BRIEF HISTORICAL OUTLOOK

Turkey as a nearly hundred-year-old republic, following the historical heritage and bonds with Ottoman Empire, has never criminalized non-heterosexual conduct or same sex relationship. Turkey as a secular and democratic state has always considered a unique example with the its Islamic nature and its strong connections with Europe and European values.

After proclamation of the Republic in 1923, many European laws and codes have been adopted. All these political reforms intended to establish a new Republic, with a secular premise. These secular steps included modernizing education, adopting Latin alphabet, equalizing women's position in public and women were given equal rights to divorce and inheritance and following these rights women became eligible to vote. Therefore, Turkey has established its Republican roots on Western values and equality from the beginning of 1923.

On the other hand, another significant element of the social life in Turkey was Islam and religious attitudes regulating everyday life and hence social life. Therefore, all laws, rules, regulations and amendments had effects on two sides. One on the political agenda and second on the society and its religious reflections. The issue of equality between men and women and in a broader view equality on different sexual orientations and LGBT people have always been issues on these two sides, a legal framework and legal rights and on the other side societal prejudice regarding strong religious commitments. Thus, this chapter intends to focus on one of these sides as legal provisions and legal codes regarding LGBT rights in Turkey, with respect to European LGBT rights and legal amendments in European Union Law. Inevitably, this intention of focusing on legal history of LGBT peoples' rights in Turkey will correspond to Turkey's candidacy to European Union and its legal requirements namely Copenhagen Criteria, including equality for everyone in front of law and human rights.

## Legal Basis of LGBT Rights in Turkey

According to European Parliament Briefing Report, in some parts of the world, negative perceptions of LGBTI[4] people are reflected in harsh laws. Consensual same-sex acts between adults are illegal in at least 72 countries, and in eight of these, they are punishable by death[5], Luckily, Turkey is not one of these countries banning non-heterosexual conduct. Arat and Nunez explain the Turkey's current state approach towards LGBTI as follows;

> *"The law in Turkey can be referred as tolerant. Non- heterosexual conduct or identity has never been criminalized and "equality before the law" and "non-discrimination" have been guiding principles for the legislative reforms undertaken since the 1990s. Thus, as far as the law is concerned, the state employs a liberal approach and tolerates "deviation". However, it does not recognize such identities and protect them. The non-discrimination clauses of the Turkish Constitution (Art. 10) and other laws (e.g Penal Code, Art. 122) omit sexual orientation and different gender identities as categories of protection. The list of protected characteristics includes "language, race, color, sex, political view, philosophical approach, religion, sect" and ends with "and similar/ other reasons," but open-ended wording of the law has never been interpreted to include "sexual orientation" or "gender identity". (Arat and Nunez, 2016: 11).*

This quotation puts two significant terms to the forefront in Turkish LGBTI legal framework; "*Tolerance*" and "*lack of legal recognition*" as two significant dimensions of LGBTI life that requires protection against

---

[4] LGBTI: Lesbian, Gay, Bisexual, Transgender and Intersex; describes a diverse group of persons who do not conform to conventional or traditional notions of male and female gender roles. LGBTI people are also sometimes referred to as 'sexual, gender and bodily minorities'.

[5] Rosamund Shreevees, European Parliament Research Center, The Rights of LGBT People in European Union, June 2018.

discrimination. Since homosexuality is still legally considered to be a mental health disorder in Turkey, expecting a legal recognition of sexual orientation in anti-discrimination law makes it less realistic.

According to Article 10 of the Turkish Constitution everyone is equal before the law and discrimination is prohibited on several grounds. However, the constitution does not explicitly protect people from discrimination on the basis of sexual orientation and gender identity[6].

Article 40 of the Turkish Civil Code provides transgender people to the right to change their sex in the official register after sex reassignment surgery. Afterwards, trans person can apply for a pink or blue identity card reflecting their self-identified gender.[7] According to Article 40 of Turkish Constitution, a person can change their gender only upon the fulfillment of specific requirements. These include obtaining a psychiatric diagnosis as well as being single, aged 18 or above and permanently incapable of reproduction.

In as many as 21 European Countries including Belgium, Finland, France, Italy, Norway and Turkey, transgender people must be sterilized to obtain legal documents that reflect their gender identity[8].

Article 90 of the Turkish Constitution stipulates that "international agreements duly put into effect have the force of law". In case of conflict, international treaties to which Turkey is party should take precedence over domestic law. In March 2012 Turkey became the first country to ratify the Council of Europe Convention on preventing and combating violence against women and domestic violence, which explicitly includes sexual orientation and gender identity as categories of non-discrimination under Art. 4(3). The protection of the rights to freedom of expression and association and the prohibition of discrimination based on sexual orientation are covered by Articles 2(1), 3 and 26 of the International Covenant on Civil and Political Rights and Articles 3, 8, 10, 14 of the European Convention on Human Rights, which Turkey has ratified. Turkey has signed but not ratified Protocol No. 12 to the European Convention on Human Rights. Article 1 of the Protocol stipulates freedom from discrimination and obliges public authorities not to discriminate.

Moreover, Turkey has obligations under the International Covenant of Economic, Social and Cultural Rights. General Comment 20 prohibits discrimination on grounds of sexual orientation and gender identity. Considering the specific international obligations to which Turkey is bound, it follows that the government should theoretically include the protection of LGBT persons under Article 90 of its Constitution or equivalent domestic

---

[6] http://www.refugeelegalaidinformation.org/turkey-lgbti-resources (Date of Access: 28.10.2018)

[7] http://www.refugeelegalaidinformation.org/turkey-lgbti-resources (Date of Access: 28.10.2018)

[8] https://assets.publishing.service.gov.uk/government/uploads/system/uploads/attachment_data/file/619683/Turkey_-_SOGI_-_CPIN_-_v2_0__June_2017_.pdf (Date of Access: 15.08.2018)

provisions[9].

Turkish Law on Protection of Family (no.4320, enacted in 1998) nor its revamped new version, the Law on Protection of the Family and Prevention of Violence against Women (no. 6284, legislated on March 8, 2012) has any references to sexual orientation and gender identity despite efforts of LGBT advocacy groups that demanded inclusion of the terms (Human Rights Violations 2012, 5) and LGBT rights are likely to be ignored in the new constitution of the country (Arat and Nunez, 2016:11). This lack of recognition in Turkish Constitution also creates an atmosphere of "*let them be*" or "*laissez-faire approach*" that LGBT people in Turkey are left by the state to enjoy the tolerance as negative freedom and this laissez-faire approach leaves what is to be tolerates to the discretion of the individual and state officials, who have power to choose to exercise discrimination and violence in the name of preserving their understanding of culture, religion, family or Turkish national character. (Arat and Nunez, 2016:11).

## The Current Situation

According to the legal basis presented above, same sex acts are not criminalized in Turkey. However, not criminalizing does not mean enjoying a full atmosphere of freedom on sexual orientation. The legal basis creates a climate of "tolerance" as Arat and Nunez also emphasized, but this tolerance does not create a climate of combat against homophobia and discrimination against LGBT people in Turkey. Demands of NGOs on LGBT rights by Kaos GL established in 1994 , SPoD established in 2011 and Lambdaistanbul established in 1993 (well-known and most organized LGBTQ Non Governmental Organizations in Turkey), were not welcomed by all governments through 2000s. LGBT organizations' demands focus on recognizing different sexual orientations in Turkish Constitution and enacting amendments on LGBT rights including expanding definitions of hate crimes against LGBT people, however, these demands were usually ignored through new Constitution making process started by 2010s.

*The rise of identity politics in the 1980s and the relative cultural and political liberalization that started in the 1990s (Arat, 2007) allowed the development of a new consciousness of gender and sexual identity and LGBT activism (Görkemli, 2014; Fishman, 2013; Bereket and Adam 2008). As LGBT groups have started to establish advocacy organizations, state officials (e.g., the office of governor in several provinces) have been trying to close them down by claiming that the mission and objectives of the LGBT organizations violate legal provisions that attempt to protect family and public morality (AI 2009 and 2010; HRW 2008) (Arat and Nunez, 2016:11).*

---

[9] http://www.refugeelegalaidinformation.org/turkey-lgbti-resources (Date of Access: 28.10.2018)

Moreover, the Turkish legal system "under-punishes" those who commit hate crimes against LGBT individuals, often imposing only small fines or minor jail time and reductions in punishments are vindicated by judges because LGBT status is considered as abnormality in the eyes of state law (Ergin, 2015:843). The perception of "*abnormality*" towards LGBT individuals usually empowered with role of religion in pre-dominantly Muslim countries like Turkey and the role of religion plays a greater intersecting role with gender and sexuality than in most Western societies, resulting in alarming levels of institutionalized discrimination (Ergin, 2015:841). High levels of discrimination also brings the lack of protection for LGBT individuals inevitably. Since it is obvious that laws do not protect LGBT people against hate crimes and LGBT identity is not a legally defined sexual identity, this puts forefront "abnormality" and "sickness" as legal perceptions of the sexual orientations in Turkey. For instance, the military specifically disapproves of gay males serving in the Turkish armed forces because it considers homosexuality as a psychosexual disorder (Ergin, 2015:4).

Understanding of same sex behavior as an abnormality or psychosexual disorder creates ostracizing of LGBT individuals in society depending on both religious, legal and social norms and values in Turkey. This ostracizing may sometimes reach to level of emotional and physical violence in society and LGBT people suffer from not only from lack of legal rights but also social acceptance. Ergin points out that as follows;

> *Individuals who fall outside the categories of the socially-accepted norms of gender binaries are ostracized, often subjected to emotional and physical violence. The data available on sexual minorities are very limited and difficult to access. This is because once LGBT individuals reveal their nonconforming gender identity or sexual orientation, their most basic rights such as the right to life, to labor, to housing, to healthcare and to education are greatly compromised (Ergin, 2015:841).*

This quotation also emphasizes the reality of excessive social pressure in the public empowered by legal lack of recognition of sexual orientation as a human right. Since legal provisions disregard the fact that different sexual orientations are "*private*" matters and concerns only individual themselves, public attitude is also directed towards "*a moral issue*" that everyone makes it their own business. Thus, many LGBT people keep their sexual orientations confidential with a fear of falling outside of socially accepted norms of society in Turkey.

## CONCLUSION

Sexual orientations are expected to become a matter of *private issues* of people in a world where human rights movement proceeds rapidly in many countries. However, LGBT reality, all over the world, does not correspond with an era of freedom and human rights. Many countries' religious or social norms and traditions usually restricts accepting the very existence of LGBT people and their sexual orientations. Thus, being an LGBT people and performing same sex behaviors are still criminalized in some countries as discussed in the text and an issue of *"private life"* comes to the forefront as a legal and social issue.

On the other hand, Western societies have been progressing more rapidly regarding LGBT rights since 1980s synchronously with European Union law making process. After Sqarcialupi Report, 1990s have brought more efforts for LGBT rights and fighting against discrimination towards LGBT people have become a significant agenda for European Union. Considering LGBT rights as a matter of human rights have matched with the European Union's agenda on developing human rights. In addition, "discrimination" has also been another significant dimension of LGBT lives and rights and combat against discrimination have been legalized in TFEU and TEU legal documents of the European Union. It is significant to point out here that, this rapid progress of the EU depends on its values that establish the Union and also bounding for Member States. As mentioned in article 2 of Treaty on European Union, *values of respect for human dignity, freedom, democracy, equality, the rule of law and respect for human rights, including the rights of persons belonging to minorities* constituted the main motives for enacting Union laws and regulations for the whole Union.

Freedom, equality and respect for human rights have strengthened the fight against discrimination against LGBT people in the EU and provided a legal basis for protecting LGBT people. This legal basis is the most crucial point of that paper, that Turkey lacks and LGBT people suffer from discrimination. Although Turkey is not a country criminalizing same sex behaviour and creates a "tolerant" approach to LGBT reality, this does not provide the essential "protection" by law. Due to religious values and norms of the country, homosexuality is not a broadly accepted sexual orientation on the contrary people are very prejudiced against LGBT people. Prejudice against LGBT people inevitably create social exclusion and ostracizing which ends up in social and physical discrimination and sometimes direct physical violence.

Turkey's LGBT activist organizations have come a long way since beginning of their establishment process from mid 1990s and become serious actors for LGBT rights. In addition, these LGBT organizations created safety zone for LGBT people where they can freely express themselves and demand their "human rights" and made LGBT people more "visible" as a unified body. However, while compared with the historical process of the LGBT rights in Western societies, Turkey still lacks main legal reforms in Constitution that will provide a "protection" rather than laissez-faire approach that was dominant until that time. Therefore, absence of the expression of *sexual orientation* in Constitution, creates ambiguous practices towards LGBT people on both state and society level.

European Union's progress on establishing a discrimination free zone for every people and each citizen disregarding their race, religion, ethnic origin and sexual orientation in every sphere of life was not an easy task to accomplish for a single state. First of all emphasis of the Unions' values as mentioned above, putting humanity, human dignity, equality respect for human rights as an inseparable part of the law, made combat against discrimination legally possible and this makes the difference between LGBT movements history in Western Europe and Turkey. Thus, an agenda on establishing a new approach on considering sexual orientation as a matter of freedom and human right may make the legal basis for equality of LGBT people more plausible in Turkey. In addition since Turkey became the first country to ratify the Council of Europe Convention on preventing and combating violence against women and domestic violence, which explicitly includes sexual orientation and gender identity as categories of non-discrimination under Art. 4(3), the protection of the rights to freedom of expression and association and the prohibition of discrimination based on sexual orientation are already protected by International law that Turkey has already been a party. Domestic law and new Constitution making process in accordance with International Treaties on LGBT rights and human rights regarding sexual orientation, is the legal basis that LGBT people in Turkey demand for decades that will strengthen fight against discrimination.

## REFERENCES

Adam, B. (1987) *The rise of a gay and lesbian movement.* Boston: Twayne Press.

Arat, Z., F. Kabasakal, C. Nunez (2016) Advancing LGBT Rights in Turkey: Tolerance or Protection?, *Human Rights Review,* DOI 10.1007/s12142-016-0439-x.

Bereket, T. and Adam, B. (2008) Navigating Islam and Same-Sex Liaisons Among Men in Turkey., *Journal of Homosexuality* 55(2):2004–222.

Arat, Z., F. Kabasakal (2007) (ed.) *Human Rights in Turkey.* Philadelphia: University of Pennsylvania Press.

Ergin, C. (2015) LGBT in Turkey: Policies and Experiences, *Social Sciences,* 2015,4, 838-858.

Fishman, L. A. (2013) Turkey and LGBT Rights: A Historical and Global Perspective, *Turkish Policy Quarterly* 11(4):149–159.

Görkemli, S. (2014) Grassroots Literacies: Lesbian and Gay Activism and the Internet in Turkey. Albany, NY: State University of New York Press.

Hantrais, L. (2007) *Social policy in the European Union.* 3rd ed. Basingstoke: Palgrave Macmillan.

Shreevees, R. (2018) The Rights of LGBT People in European Union, *European Parliament Research Center Briefing Report.*

Swiebel, J. (2009) Lesbian, gay, bisexual and transgender human rights: the search for an international strategy, Contemporary Politics, 15:1, 19-35, DOI: 10.1080/13569770802674196

Kollman, K. and M. Waites (2009) The global politics of lesbian, gay, bisexual and transgender human rights: an introduction, *Contemporary Politics*, 15:1, 1-17, DOI: 10.1080/13569770802674188

Waaldijk, K. (2000) Civil developments: patterns of reform in the legal position of same-sex partners in Europe. *Canadian Journal of Family Law*, 17 (1), 62–64.

INTERNET RESOURCES

Amnesty International. 2009. Turkish LGBT organization wins appeal against closure. https://www.amnesty.org/en/latest/news/2009/01/turkish-lgbt-organization-wins-appeal-against-closure-20090121 (Date of Access: 15.10.2016).

HRW (Human Rights Watch). 2008. We Need a Law for Liberation: Gender, Sexuality, and Human Rights in a Changing Turkey. https://www.hrw.org/sites/default/files /reports/ turkey0508webwcover.pdf (Date of Access: 16.10.2016)

https://europadatenbank.iaaeu.de/user/view_legalact.php?id=254 (Date of Access: 28.10.2018)

http://www.refugeelegalaidinformation.org/turkey-lgbti-resources (Date of Access: 28.10.2018)

https://assets.publishing.service.gov.uk/government/uploads/system/uploads/attachment _data/file/619683/Turkey_-_SOGI_-_CPIN_-_v2_0__June_2017_.pdf (Date of Access: 15.08.2018)

# CHAPTER 3

# TRANS WOMEN PRISONERS IN TURKEY[1]

Selin Berghan

## INTRODUCTION

Studies on trans prisoners are quite rare in spite of the steady increase in the number of studies and researches on LGBTI in recent years. Though there is some increase in the number of studies on LGBTI in general and trans prisoners in particular, these studies still remain quite limited both internationally and in Turkey. LGBTI individuals are often unprotected in the judicial system from discrimination and violence on the basis of their sexual identity and orientation. While some trans women and gay prisoners can conceal their identity, "excessive" visibility of trans women increases the risk of maltreatment and violence (ACLU&NCLR 2014; UNODC 2009). Further, those who are perceived as gay though not being so, may also face the same forms of violence.

Several international mechanisms oblige States to protect all prisoners. Also, States are expected to engage in positive action to eliminate all forms of discrimination that "prisoners with special needs" including LGBTI may face (UNODC 2009).

In this context, the present report seeks to expose the experience and needs of trans women in Turkish prisons on the basis of correspondence between the Pembe Hayat (Pink Life) LGBTT Solidarity Association[2] and 67 trans women in the period of 2008-2016. The prison experience of trans women as reflected in their letters is approached on the basis of violations they suffer and in terms of their needs. 6 of the women in the group are of foreign nationality. These persons face double risk for their sexual identity and also alien status and these risks are addressed under a separate heading in this report. The report ends with some suggestions relating to the strengthening of the justice system, prevention of discrimination, and equal

---

[1] This report first prepared and published in Turkish by Pink Life. It is being republished with the permission of Pink Life.

[2] The first and the largest trans* self-organization in Turkey, established in 2006.

treatment to all prisoners.

## CONTENT, PURPOSE AND METHODOLOGY OF THE REPORT

The present report is intended to expose and analyse the experience and needs of trans woman prisoners in Turkish prisons from the perspective of international human rights framework, and to develop suggestions. The analysis is essentially based on problems identified in the "Handbook on Prisoners with Special Needs" (2009) prepared by the UN Office on Drugs and Crime and complemented by data and outcomes present in few other reports and studies available in Turkey. The problems can be basically described as transphobia in judiciary and prison processes, threat of sexual violence, discriminatory practices of relevant institutions, health problems, and social isolation.

There is no information concerning the number of trans prisoners in Turkish prisons. Upon the application of the Civil Society Association on Penal Execution System (CISST) for information made in May 2014, it was stated that there were 95 LGBTI prisoners in prisons, but no information was given as to their distribution by prisons and ratio of LGBTIs. The 2015 application of the CISST remained without any response on the basis of the "right to privacy" (CISST 2015). Public institutions do not respond to applications made for purposes of obtaining information since the start of state of emergency in 2016. Hence, there is no information as to how many LGBTI prisoners are incarcerated in Turkish prisons.

The present report essentially is based on letters received by Pink Life from trans women in prisons. The efforts for solidarity with trans prisoners, which started in 2008 with the imprisonment of the Association's chairperson Buse Kılıçkaya, gained a more systematic character with the launching of "Dress Bank" in the memory of Dilek İnce who fell victim to hate murder in 2014.

Letters included in the report:

- The correspondences with 67 trans women made in the period 2008-2016 are included in the report.
- There were multiple correspondences with 38 of these persons. There are some prisoners with whom over 20 letters were exchanged. There was single correspondence with 29 prisoners with whom the Pembe Hayat corresponded regarding their needs under the Dress Bank facility.
- Correspondence with trans women became systematic with the Dilek İnce Dress Bank and 150 letters were responded to during the period 2014-2016.

- 6 of these persons are of foreign nationality (5 Brazilians and 1 with Azeri origin).
- Only one of these prisoners has undergone sex reassignment surgery and is an inmate in a women's prison. The rest, 66 persons are kept in prisons for men.
- Of these persons 7 have been in more than one prison while one has been in 8 different prisons for various reasons.
- While there are some prisoners giving information on this issue, the Pembe Hayat does not ask them what they were charged with as a matter of Association policy. It can be said that some trans prisoners in correspondence have few months as their remaining terms of prisonment; there are some others who were sentenced to life imprisonment.
- 6 persons were released during the correspondence period.
- Letters included in the report come from 14 cities and 18 prisons.

It can be listed as follows:

- Afyon
- Adana – Kürkçüler
- Ankara – Sincan
- Antalya
  - Alanya
- Bolu
- Çorum
- Eskişehir
- İzmir – Menemen
- İstanbul
  - Ümraniye
  - Maltepe
  - Bakırköy
  - Metris
- Kocaeli
  - Men's prison
  - Women's prison
- Osmaniye
- Rize – Kalandere
- Samsun – Bafra
- Tekirdağ

## Dilek İnce Dress Bank

The Dilek İnce Dress Bank established by Pink Life on 20 November

2014 on the occasion of the Transgender Day of Remembrance derives its name from trans woman Dilek İnce who was killed with a pump-rifle during the Eryaman events in 2006.

The Dilek İnce Dress Bank functions as a network of solidarity by means of contributions from volunteers. The bank collects clean and usable dresses from its volunteers and sends them to needy refugee and imprisoned LGBTIs in line with demands as stated in letters sent to Pink Life, KAOS-GL and Civil Society Association on Penal Execution System. Dress support to imprisoned LGBTIs is made four times in eachyear. Since its start, the Dilek İnce Dress Bank has made 10 such supports in bulk. While the first support given in 2014 reached 30 prisoners, the support in March 2016 covered 70 persons.

Trans prisoners can find information about and communicate with Pink Life and the Bank through other trans prisoners or the psychologist of their facility. Pink Life regularly communicates with psychologists working in prisons and informs them about the Dilek İnce Dress Bank.

In the period 2008-2010 the Pink Life pursued various activities in the name of trans women in need and tried to extend material support in this way. Besides, the association also tries to support the production of handmade items made by prisoners such as bead and knitting work by marketing and supplying necessary materials. The need for material support, however, still remains as an important problem.

The following are some kinds of dresses and personal items demanded in letters and provided by the Dilek İnce Dress Bank:

- Summer and winter clothes (t-shirt, pants, dress, skirts, tight, coat, reefer jacket, sweats, etc.)
- Underwear, supported bra in particular
- Summer and winter shoes, heeled ones in particular
- Slippers
- Towel
- Quilt cover, blanket
- Washcloth
- Bijouterie (ring, necklace, earring, bracelet) (cannot be metal)
- Makeup materials (eye shadow, blusher, face powder, hail polish, acetone, lipstick, cream) (in unopened containers)
- Wig

Others apart from personal objects demandedand met are as follows:

- Sources of information (information about sexual reassignment surgery, books and periodicals, addresses of other LGBTI associations).

- Religious items (prayer rug, rosary).

## NATIONAL AND INTERNATIONAL STANDARDS

### National Legislation

Being LGBTI is not an offence in Turkey, but there is no specific legislation protecting LGBTI individuals from discrimination. In spite of the Turkish State's commitment to guarantee equality and prevent discrimination as a party to conventions mentioned below and under Constitutional Article no. 10, the actual situation is not so and there is no provision in any legislation referring to "sexual identity and sexual orientation."

### International Standards

Although there is no special rule that apply to LGBT prisoners, all provisions included the ones mentioned below apply to all detainees and prisoners without discrimination (UNODC 2009). In other words, LGBTI prisoners are entitled to the same rights as others and there are many international mechanisms guaranteeing these rights.

- The Universal Declaration of Human Rights, articles 2, 3, 5, 7, 9, 12.
- International Covenant on Civil and Political Rights, articles 2, 6, 7, 9, 17, 26.
- Yogyakarta Principles on the Application of International Human Rights Law in relation to Sexual Orientation and Gender Identity, principle 9.
- International Covenant on Economic, Social and Cultural Rights, article 2.
- UN Convention against Torture and other Cruel, Inhuman or Degrading Treatment of Punishment
- UN Standard Minimum Rules for the Treatment of Prisoners and the Body of Principles for the Protection of All Persons under Any Form of Detention or Imprisonment
- Basic Principles for the Treatment of Prisoners
- Standard Minimum Rules for the Treatment of Prisoners
- European Convention on Human Rights

## PRISON EXPERIENCE OF TRANS WOMEN

### Access to Justice

The problems of trans woman prisoners regarding the access to justice start before they enter into the criminal justice system. They are "offenders" per se for their trans identity. Though having LGBTI identity is not a legal offence in Turkey, discrimination against LGBTI individuals in general and trans women in particular is a concrete fact in all spheres of life. Studies too show that trans women in this country are the "other of the others". Rejection by family, bullying and exclusion faced in schools and discrimination in working life force trans women to a style of life that involves risky behaviour. Hence, cases where trans women are perpetrators are in fact directly related to discrimination they face (MAP 2016; Koyuncu 2015; CISST 2015) and the main cause of acts for which they are imprisoned is their deprivation of life safety and means of subsistence (CİSST 2016).

Violence against trans women is justified, and the state of being trans is considered as a rationale for penalty remission even in cases of homicide (Pembe Hayat and KAOS GL, 2013, 2015; KAOS GL 2013). Court cases where trans women are perpetrators are concluded faster than similar others (CISST 2015, 2016). In other words the guilt of trans women is proven quicker than all others in this country.

Prior to court process, they suffer from secondary victimization at the hands of maltreating security officers in police stations. The problems they face in access to justice and in due process include the following: Authorities not taking their statements seriously; their complaints about security forces remaining ineffective; absence in court sessions of lawyers appointed by bar associations for those unable to hire lawyers; discriminatory attitudes of judges that influence court decisions of imprisonment; and having their complaints to prison managements go without any response (UNODC 2009, Koyuncu 2015, CISST 2015, 2016).

Further, trans prisoners are in need of information and support on such matters as their rights and responsibilities as prisoners, their files still in process or referred to the Court of Appeal, and procedures for filing complaints about violations and discrimination they may face in prisons. This information is either not given at all or given only randomly.

*"We are blamed on only for the life we have chosen, for our free way of life."*

*"The court decision was absolutely unethical and unlawful, deriving from grudge and hatred of my identity. The court did not consider remission factors supported by concrete evidence and spoke scornfully to may face using the discourse "those like you."... I was tried not as a normal person who is suspected of some deed, but plainly as a disgusting and despicable one."*

*"We are in the mouth of crocodile. Anyone who wants can start chewing us because they have their untouchable status. No prosecutor, no judge, neither the Minister of Justice nor a court touches them. That is why prison managements commit so many crimes against humanity."*

*"I lost the rest of my family in the 1999 Earthquake. I have nobody outside... I was alone drifting from one prison to6 another. My hard days going on since then... We have been pushed around, looked upon with content, regarded as 3rd class people..."*

*"I am 30 years old and I am in prison for 11 months now. They gave me life imprisonment for a crime I did not actually commit but assumed upon the deception of one of my relatives... I appear as a woman. Not all in my family know I am a trans... My family sends me man's clothes, but I can't wear them."*

*"Whatever I say from here will sound alien. Inside or outside makes no difference for us. We are born to bread without salt. Outside you have the pressure of what they call society, and here you have the pressure of other prisoners. As a trans individual there are times you are afraid of being free while in prison..."*

## DENIAL OF SEXUAL IDENTITY

Prisons are facilities designed on the basis of two sexes. It means persons are placed in men's or women's prisons according to their genital organs. This exclusionist practice does not recognize the sexual identity of trans women who have not undergone or do not want to undergo reassignment surgery. Trans women are placed in men's prisons designed according to men's needs. This situation leads to many violations of the rights of trans women and increases the risk of exposure to violence.

Trans women sent to men's prisons are searched upon arrival by male officials despite their objection. This search is conducted by both guardians and military personnel in some cases, almost always with insults and scornful comments, and incomers are stripped naked although it is unlawful.

According to the legislation in effect[1] naked body search can be done only in cases where "there are reasonable and serious indications that the convict has on some substance or item forbidden to be brought into the institution and when deemed necessary by the highest authority in the institution." When it comes to trans women naked search is conducted with no regard to relevant rules and in a way against human dignity.

The denial of sexual identity continues inside with insistent attitudes of prison officials calling trans prisoners with their male names appearing in their identification or using such attributions like "*nonoş*" as a means of insult. Also, the refusal of such requests of trans women as mirrors and tweezers,

---

[1]Article 46 of the Regulations on the Management of Penitentiary Institutions and Execution of Penalties and Security Measures.

imposition to wear men's clothes, forcing them to live "as males", and compulsory haircuts add up to the denial of sexual identity. Unavailability in prison canteens of clothes and personal items mentioned in letters and, even when available, high pricing of low quality items is another problem.

Besides personal items, some other important ones like ward electricity connection, cleaning materials like soap and detergent, tea, boiler, TV, etc. have to be procured from the prison canteen as well. Many trans woman prisoners cannot meet their families. Unless they have some money of their own or support of someone out of prison, they are financially strandedand mostly unable to provide for their basic needs since they are not allowed to work in İŞKUR (Turkish Employment Agency) workshops in prisons for security reasons.

## SOLITARY CONFINEMENT AS A SECURITY MEASURE

Trans prisoners need to be protected from the sexual harassment and violence of other prisoners (UNODC 2009). The solution found in Turkish prisons is to keep trans women alone in their cells and to ban their presence in commonly used yards and participation to some joint activities, which means isolation. For reasons allegedly related to safety trans women prisoners can be kept isolated and denied the right to participate in sports activities, İŞKUR (TurkeyEmployement Agency) workshops, and education-training that other prisoners are entitled to.

It is unlawful that prisoners are kept single in their cells without any punitive decision of solitary confinement. It can be added that Turkey was convicted by the ECHR on the case of a gay prisoners kept single in a cell for 8 months (CİSST 2016). Yet, keeping single in cells has become a rule especially when there is no other trans person in the prison. These prisoners further face limitations or bans when exercising rights that all prisoners are entitled to.

*"For 2 years they have been keeping me alone in a room as if a hostage for my sexual identity. They isolate me saying that it is for my safety. They convert any problem or need into a torture."*

*"I was kept in isolation in many prisons I served my term earlier because of my sexual identity. I have documents confirming this situation of mine, I expect to be released."*

*"At present we are kept in single-inmate cells in the same block. We are altogether 10 inmates on the first and second floor. "*

*"We are 8-10 people here. But each of us is kept separate from others. Our penalty is executed singularly. In other words it is like a box with no outlet. Believe me we are all bad in psychological terms. I feel terrible, we all do. I wouldn't mind it if my terms was short, but I have 1.5 years to go. Will it remain so?"*

*"Can you just think of it? I have one 1 a day to go out to the yard. It is as if I am in solitary confinement without any such sanction. I wouldn't so bad if it were. All I want is to get out of this 90-steps room and serve my term in better conditions."*

*"I am a trans woman. But yet without my pink identity they take my old name as valid. I am in prison for a long time and here in this prison for the last one year. I suffer discrimination in its worst form for being Kurdish and travesty at the same time. Since I arrived here I am being kept alone in a cell like a captive or hostage. They say, "You either stay alone or together with your adversary, the person who assaulted you." They don't let anybody stay with me and go out to some commonly used places. For 8 months they didn't let me out to any other place. After 8 months they let me out alone for sports. In the F-type prison, on the other hand, I had the right to 9 hours of outdoor activity a week."*

*"We cannot take part in any prison activity leaving aside sports. Fortnightly we go out to gymnasium for an hour, but we play volleyball every day in our ward."*

*"We are getting to be a group here. There are 17 trans persons now. Though we have no problem in-between they don't let us out together for social activities."*

In some cases, trans prisoners commit disciplinary breaches either for non-response to their requests like tweezers or for being placed in confinement due to safety reasons. They are unprotected against the discriminatory treatment, insults and threats of violence by prison personnel and management. Their petitions to public prosecutor's office are not processed by prison managements. Adding these arbitrary dispositions, violence and maltreatment and confinement together, trans women start hunger strikes or attempt suicide to have their voices heard.

*"Insults, curses, contempt… I got used to other prisoners and I don't pay heed, but what about those public servants? I cannot have any complaint petition reach official authorities."*

*"Life is playing its game to us. The fate of many trans women in prisons is the same.*

*We are confronted with different kinds of problems each day. No single day passes here without its problems. We are serving punishment within punishment. We are 10 in this prison now and we share the same ward."*

*They solve no problem of mine, they do not respond to my petitions and needs, my petitions and letters are not sent to their addresses, they are withheld. "*

*"I have exhausted my resilience. I started hunger strike. The response they gave was 'You will stay alone until your term is over."*

The latest form of isolation that trans women experience is the denial of their sexual identity by their families. There are very few trans prisoners still in contact with their families. Their families are either unaware of their sexual identity or take it as homosexuality. The rest are rejected by their families due to their sexual identity and so they are not visited. Those who are kept in prisons located in places other than their usual living places cannot visited by their friends too. This means a state of extreme desolateness and seclusion in a sense.

## RIGHT TO HEALTH

The leading health-related need of trans women in prison is psychological support because of the contempt, violence, isolation, prison conditions, loneliness and feeling of desperation they experience. In addition to this it is also important to start or continue hormone use and having sexual reassignment surgery for some.

The socio-psychological support given in prisons is not sufficient in some cases and may even be harmful since the personnel concerned lack necessary information and experience concerning trans prisoner or have their specific prejudices. Since there is no standard in the provision of this service good practices remain rare. It comes to mean a great support for the trans prisoner in cases where the prison psychologist has no prejudice.

Trans prisoners may continue using hormone depending on the attitude of prison personnel, particularly those in charge of health affairs. While there are some who start using hormone in prison, there are also others whose hormonal therapy is prevented. As to sexual reassignment surgery, it is possible if the prisoner has means for it, but not considered as a part of the right to health in prisons.

*"They sent me here from Bolu saying 'You are exiled, they will ruin you there', but my God is so great and benevolent that this prison what they called 'exile' turned out to be so good for me. The psychologist here in Eskişehir H-type closed prison is such a nice*

*woman. The facility is very good. The management, management staff, wardens, the doctor and other personnel are also very nice persons. I wish I could be here earlier so I'd have avoided those disciplinary penalties… So far you have made dozens of publications on prisons where LGBTs were kept. If you ever have any new publication on the issue, could you mention the psychologist, doctor, wardens and the teacher on duty here in this prison? That they are so nice to us LGBTIs to the extent not letting us depressed by prison psychology?"*

*"I have been in prison for long years. I started hormone therapy two years ago."*

*"No hormone therapy or any other healthcare for me. They give me anaesthetic, passing-out pills instead of hormone. That so-called doctor tells me 'I give no therapy to you, go and make your complaint to anybody you can…'"*

*"I was anxious while coming here expecting similar problems and difficulties. But the psychologist of the facility turned out to be a kind-hearted woman as it was the case back in Eskişehir. Different than many others, she is not malevolent, prejudiced and transphobic."*

## FOREIGN TRANS WOMEN PRISONERS

In recent years, increased migration as a consequence of armed conflicts and offences like human and drug trafficking it brings along, the number of prisoners of foreign nationality has increased both globally and in Turkey (UNODC 2009).

Problems that prisoners of foreign nationality face in the judicial system include difficulties steaming from language barriers, lack of information about rights, being separated from their families and feeling of isolation, discrimination, not being able to benefit from their rights to vocational and other trainings, and enjoying only limited material support (UNODC 2009).

Since 2010, 6 trans women of foreign nationality, 5 Brazilians and 1 Azeri from İstanbul Maltepe, Bilecik and Çorum prisons have reached the Pembe Hayat Association with their letters. These women staying in the same ward with other women prisoners have enjoyed the material and moral support of their inmates, learned about and benefitted from the Dress Bank, and learned Turkish. They are also in communication with their respective Consulates. But they say their consulates were not as supportive as they hoped or expected except for limited material support they receive in every 6 months. Thus their main support comes from trans women of Turkey with whom they stay. However, upon a new arrangement introduced in 2015 trans women of foreign nationality were transferred to wards reserved for foreigners.

*"I am in Maltepe closed prison and I am from Brazil. As a Brazilian I have no acquaintance in Turkey and I need your help. I am writing down our needs together with friends here…"*

*"We need a Portuguese-Turkish dictionary. There is now another friend from Brazil staying in another ward and not speaking Turkish. This friend has hearing problem and uses earphone, but since the device is not working she cannot hear well. I want you to help this friend as well. It is better if you send a dictionary big enough because my friend cannot read small letters. Thank you very much."*

*"We received dresses and shoes, we all liked them and very happy about it. Can you keep helping and supporting us? Thank you very much for dictionaries too, it is good that we learn Turkish day by day…"*

*"I am in my cell and in a terrible mood. The Ministry of Justice separated Turkish travesties from travesties of other nationalities. We don't know why. We stay in L-type prison no.3 while Turkish travesties are in L-type prison no.1. We are 5 here and we want to be together with our Turkish friends. I don't eat for 2 days; I mean I am on hunger strike. I will continue until my Turkish friends go there… It is a foreign prison for us. We and other men of foreign nationalities stay here under difficult circumstances. Other travesties here stay apart because we cannot get along well. There are those among Turkish travesties who are economically better off. We used to get along well with them and get socialized. I cried so much that no more tears come off. I am really bad and about to go mad."*

*"Our situation is too bad. Maltepe prison no.3 is not fit for us. We are victimized here. Even a dog would not stay in the place where I am now. This place is not for us. Only god knows our pain and suffering. Our psychology is utterly disturbed. It was much better when we were together with our gay Turkish friends. The favour I ask from you is not to let us alone in this prison. Send us back to our friends. I swear we are dying here. It is absolutely wrong to keep us here in cells since we are given no such penalty."*

*"We want to stay together with our gay friends. I am now separated in a cell for 10 month. I don't feel good psychologically. We are from Brazil and we want to stay together. They are now staying with men but they don't want it. We want to be together."*

*"For how long can I stay alone? It impossible for me to serve 30 years and 6 months all alone. I am all alone here with nobody to speak to. I don't deserve this. Is it a crime to be LGBT? There are 10 of us in Maltepe L-type prison. There are 5 in Maltepe prison no.3. My friends used to respond to all my needs. Now I cannot eat well, I drink tap water; meals are too bad and this prison is not good for us. I had a stutter in my case. I stayed in Bakırköy Hospital for 50 days. May stutter gets even worse when there is nobody to speak to."*

## CONCLUSION AND SUGGESTIONS

Trans women face discrimination and violence in their family, school and working life, which drive them to risky behaviour. In order to prevent these discriminatory practices and violence that trans women experience in all spheres of life and to combat transphobia, firstly the terms "sexual orientation" and "sexual identity" must be incorporated into legislation dealing with issues of equality and anti-discrimination.

In the judiciary system, trans women are also confronted with discriminatory practices and violence by security forces and judges. To combat transphobia and homophobia in the judiciary system there is need to train all personnel in topics of sexual orientation and sexual identity. Further, relevant regulations must have provisions envisaging the penalization of public personnel who are engaged in discriminatory acts in this regard. Similar trainings must also cover prison management staff and personnel and overall standards must be developed to stress that no discrimination can be made on the basis of sexual identity and sexual orientation.

The practice of naked search during first placement in prison must be immediately terminated. Besides being a humiliating act, it is also against the law.

Trans women are entitled to the same rights as other prisoners (i.e. health, sports activities, open prison, outdoor spaces, employment in İŞKUR jobs, etc.) and they cannot be deprived of these rights arbitrarily or for so called security reasons.

As all other prisoners, trans prisoners must be given health check-up while being taken in and enjoy healthcare services on equal terms with others. Also, hormone therapy as a special need and, if preferred, sexual reassignment surgeries must be provided for.

Mechanisms compatible with human rights and dignity must be developed instead of confinement practices based on security considerations. There must be programmes to protect trans and all other prisoners from sexual and other forms of assault accompanied by accessible and effective mechanisms of complaint for cases of assault.

For trans women of foreign nationality, they must be provided opportunities of unimpeded contact with their consulates and families, informed about their rights in their native languages; their needs in learning Turkish, reading books in foreign languages in libraries, religious practices and nutrition must be met.

Civil society organizations must keep in solidarity with their letters and visits, and contribute to efforts to make visible and prevent violations and violence in prisons through their reporting and monitoring activities. Prison visits and related activities of civil society organizations must be facilitated by the Ministry of Justice and prison managements.

# REFERENCES

ACLU & NCLR. (2014) "Know Your Rıghts: Laws, Court Decisions, and Advocacy Tips toProtect Transgender Prisoners". https://www.aclu.org/files/assets/121414-aclu-prea-kyrs-1_copy.pdf.

Black&Pink. (2015) "Coming Out Of Concrete Closets: A Report On Black & Pink's National LGBTQ Prisoner Survey". http://www.blackandpink.org/wp-content/upLoads/Coming-Out-of-Concrete-Closets.-Black-and-Pink.-October-21-2015..pdf.

BM Uyuşturucu ve Suç ile Mücadele Ofisi. (2009) "Özel İhtiyaçlara Sahip Mahpuslar Üzerine Elkitabı". In Turkish: CİSST.

Center for American Progress. (2016) "Unjust: How The Broken Criminal Justice System Fails LGBT People", http://www.lgbtmap.org/file/lgbt-criminal-justice.pdf.

CİSST. (2016) "Hapishanede Engelli, Yabancı, LGBTT Olmak: Özel İhtiyaçları Olan Mahpuslar ve İlgili Sivil Toplum Örgütleri Ağı Projesi Raporu". Report by Zeynep Alpar. https://ozelihtiyaclimahpuslar.wordpress.com/2014-2015-ozel-ihtiyaclari-olanmahpuslar-raporu/.

CİSST. (2015) "Voltaçark: Hapiste LGBTİ Olmak". Ed. Rosida Koyuncu. https://ozelihtiyaclimahpuslar.wordpress.com/tag/rosida-koyuncu/.

CİSST. (2015) "Hapiste Engelli, Yabancı, LGBTİ Olmak". Konferans Kitabı. https://ozelihtiyaclimahpuslar.wordpress.com/konferans-kitabi-hapishanedeengelli-yabanci-lgbti-olmak/.

https://ozelihtiyaclimahpuslar.wordpress.com/bm-ozel-ihtiyaclara-sahip-mahpuslar-el-kitabi/.

IPRT. (2016) "Out on the Inside: The Rights, Experiences and Needs of LGBT People in Prison". http://webcache.googleusercontent.com/search?q=cache:1wRXQIX3mzUJ:www.iprt.ie/files/IPRT_Out_on_the_Inside_2016_EMBARGO_TO_1030_Feb_02_2016.pdf+&cd=1&hl=tr&ct=clnk&gl=tr&client=safari

Kaos GL. (2013) "2013 yılında Türkiye'de Gerçekleşen Homofobi ve Transfobi Temelli Nefret Suçları Raporu". Ankara.

Pembe Hayat & Kaos GL. (2013) "2013 Cinsel Yönelim ve Cinsiye Kimliği Temelli İnsan Hakları İzleme Raporu".

# CHAPTER 4

# OTHERS IN MEDIA: LGBT INDIVIDUALS[1]

Yasemin Giritli İnceoğlu

In Turkish media, the representation of homosexuality is roughly categorized in three periods. "Homosexuals" were perceived as abnormal and "an imaginary creature" after the coup d'état on September 12, 1980. Homosexuals appeared on media as individuals relating to murders, immorality, anal sex, prostitution, transsexual in slang, AIDS, and a bad example for kids in society. After the formula which homosexuality equals to transvestite and transsexuality was dominated in the first period, the lack of self-confidence in the period of visibility on media raised doubts about media. "Half-masked" would not be wrong to say for this period. In the second period, Kaos GL (Kaos Gay and Lesbian Cultural Research and Solidarity Association) issued the first magazine on gays and lesbians in Turkey in 1994. In addition to this magazine, Express periodical magazine and Cumhuriyet daily of the year gave coverage to LGBT movement. Eventually, the third period may be defined as "unmasked." On May 1, 2001, Kaos GL freely and confidently remonstrated with labors and students by holding a banner on which "we are homosexuals, we are real and here" was written. The current situation is as is known to all. Although media is generally seen as shifted from apprenticeship to mastership on making news about LGBT individuals, they sometimes report or broadcast extremely sensitively, but they occasionally get out of kilter by giving headlines such as "They seized after getting out gay bar", "Transvestite Violance", "Homosexual Murder", "I killed because he asked me anal sex," "Transvestites bargain for prostitution on streets."

The representation of LGBT individuals in media is notably problematic. Within the scope of this representation which may be summarized as a reflection of homophobic, sexist and patriarchal structure on media, LGBT individuals are reported as news by identifying with sexuality and crime, by featuring their sexual orientation and/or gender identities, and sometimes by

---

1 This review is a revised version of preface published in the book titled with "Masculinity in Offside: Football, Homosexuality and the Story of Halil İbrahim Dinçdağ" by Burcu Karakaş and Bawer Çakır in 2013.

caricaturing. For example, a headline like "gay thief" is possibly brought out in mainstream media. While the sexual orientation of a thief is not newsworthy or heterosexuality of a thief is not regarded as necessary, specifying the sexual orientation is quite wrong. In this respect, the approach shown by Reuters seems as a guiding light: "The race, color, ethnicity, religion, sexual orientation of an individual is only specified when the subject matter is related to it."

News affirming the violence turned to LGBT individuals or showing the violence as deserved are available and reported on media. Hate speech related to sexual orientation is placed among the third page news in almost all newspapers. The language is imprecisely used, and headlines and contents consist of negative meanings. News about LGBT is framed within the scope of crime, violence, and immorality. LGBT individuals are discriminated because they are deviant. This should be considered as part of hate speech because the language of news creates the infrastructure of violence. The violence is legitimated with traditions, social beliefs, humbling cliches.

İdris Naim Şahin, former Minister of Internal Affairs, said "Homosexuality is a dishonest, immoral and inhuman fact." In addition to this, Aliye Kavaf, former Minister of State Responsible for Women and Family Affairs, came up with an explanation like "Homosexuality is an illness." Both statements are discriminatory because they consist of prejudice, extremism, and negativity. They are unfortunate with regards to more importantly including vital disinformation. Mrs. Kavaf thinks of homosexuality as a curable illness with psychotherapy and antidepressants: however, homosexuality was no longer listed as a category of disorder by American Psychological Association in 1973, and World Health Organization (WHO) on May 17th, 1990. In addition to this, "No person may be forced to undergo any form of medical or psychological treatment based on sexual orientation" was emphasized in the 18th principle in Yogyakarta Principles.

On the other hand, people making fun of "raping lesbians in order to be reintroduced to society" on the pages of social networking sites can only be seen as a hopeless case. These ideas are not different from the statements on homosexuality as an illness. Raping lesbians in order to bring them into line reveals a serious pathological state. Except that, there are people believing in it wholeheartedly and seeing it as a suggestion for the solution. These people cannot quite simply get well as too little too late.

In Turkey, a research was carried out to make us form an opinion about the general perception in public. A question like "Who would you not want to be neighbors with?" was asked to 1715 individuals in 34 cities as part of the research titled with "Radicalism and Extremism" by Prof. Dr. Yılmaz Esmer in 2009. 87% of the participants answered this question with "homosexuals." This result says a lot about how hard LGBT individuals maintain their lives in Turkey.

As seen in the argument used for Vejdeland v. Sweden case which European Court of Human Rights judged the discourse targeting homosexuals, the notion "racism" has been used as an umbrella term covering all the discriminatory motives. European Court of Human Rights handed down in the case of Vejdeland v. Sweden: "The court reiterates that inciting to hatred does not necessarily entail a call for an act of violence, or other criminal acts. Attacks on persons committed by insulting, holding up to ridicule or slandering specific groups of the population can be sufficient for the authorities to favor combating racist speech in the face of freedom of expression exercised in an irresponsible manner. In this regard, the Court stresses that discrimination based on sexual orientation is as serious as discrimination based on race, origin or color."

The States, Spain, the Netherlands, Belgium, Norway and South Africa legalized same sex marriages: on the other hand, homosexual partners are legally entitled in Finland, France, the UK, Denmark, Switzerland, Germany, Portugal, Iceland and New Zealand. As that being the case in EU countries, one of which Turkey is as a candidate country, the political power cannot remain unresponsive for a long period of time. I think that there is a need of initiative on this case as the other initiatives are embarked on.

As is known, Hate Crimes Bill was prepared by Hate Crimes Law Campaign Platform. In this bill, hate crime is defined as crimes perpetrated with hate motives against anybody or any specific group because of their race, ethnicity, color, religion, language, gender, sexual orientation, gender identity, physical or mental disorder, the state of health or age. The bill consists of the crimes with hate motives such as homicide, intentional injury, torture, sexual assault, threat, child abuse, offenses against liberty, offenses against freedom of religion, thought and belief, violation of residence immunity, unlawful search, plundering, damage to property, damaging places of worship and cemeteries, intentionally risking general safety, threats to cause fear and panic.

In hate crimes, the offender purposely aims at the victim because of his/her key and indispensable feature which s/he represent or s/he is thought as representing. In Penal Code, the overall tendency to make a decision on a crime is based on paying regard to the motives behind it. According to Article 82 - 1 - k in the Penal Code of Turkey no. 5237, the act of intentional killing with the motive of tradition is sentenced as major offense.

Hate Crimes Law is available in 48 countries of 56 in the Organization for Security and Co-operation in Europe, and Turkey is one of the rest which does not lay it down. Turkey, as one of the countries in the Organization for Security and Co-operation in Europe, acknowledged and undertook on qualifying its own regulations, gathering data, guaranteeing to ascertain and prosecute hate crimes, and providing trainings when needed - as done in the other countries. In the circumstances, this bill should be passed by all the items mentioned above.

Making legal regulations or law is not sufficient without doubt. As done in European countries or the States, data should be collected and publicly shared in Turkey. In addition to this, trainings for jurisdiction and media professionals, and regulations providing support to rehabilitate victims are needed. In this respect, an important part of this mission falls to the media. The power of words and images should be appropriately used on media in order to maintain mutual understanding, respect, inter-identical/-cultural dialogue.

The latest news is worrisome. Constitution Conciliation Committee in Turkish Grand National Assembly reached a compromise on stating "sexual orientation and gender identity" not in the article, but in its legislative intention. This is not political or legal binding. The article - as it is stated - leaves the responsibility and mercy of judiciary members for tackling homophobia- and transphobia-based violation of rights. At this point, I want to emphasize that considerable steps on LGBT right campaigns have been taken, and we should be optimistic about its future.

# CHAPTER 5

# SOCIAL MEDIA USE IN LGBTQI MOVEMENTS IN TURKEY

Sinan Aşçı

To deepen our understanding of the relationship between social media and political movements since 2013 when Gezi Park Protests sparked as a wave of demonstrations and civil unrest in Turkey, events must have been situated in a larger context of media use and recent history of online activism. Since that day, the most successful social movements in Turkey were those using social media to expand networks of disaffected people, broker relations between activists, and globalize the resources. By this way, social media afforded those people the means to shape repertoires of contention, frame the issues, propagate unifying symbols, and transform online activism into offline protests. Because of being apparently excluded in all the forms of mass media, dissenting voices tend to form alternative spheres creating a different public sphere, a type of public sphere which is increasing the possibilities for a public articulation of experience. As a way of "survey research," social media accounts of LGBTQI NGOs in Twitter, as an online public sphere, were observed in a meta analysis way. Data collected from this first-hand observation was evaluated with the help of content analysis techniques. The survey sample was designated with these accounts' names, number of posts, followers, and other/optional information stated in the accounts specifically belonging to the platform. Based on the data, this chapter aims to analyze what LGBTQI individuals generate for resistance, and how they have used social media in their movements since 2013, precisely based on the use of social media platform mentioned above during Pride Weeks in subjected years. The findings shed light on the social media use and habits of LGBTQI communities.

## INTRODUCTION

Daily life is almost completely changed based on the developments in communication and information technologies, which differs in societies' accessibility. With the most recent information and communication technologies, hereafter called ICTs[1], and their links via WWW[2] (the Internet), citizen groups in the societies and their social movements, like many other organizations and institutions, are likely to reach a new level in the ways in which they mobilize, build coalitions, inform, lobby, communicate, and campaign (Hajnal, 2002). The tools of communication in social movements seem to be changed with high-tech and/or mobile ones in contemporary forms, not only as a part of these movements but also a tool used by the actors involved in the movements.

Social movements have been seen on the stage as "labor movements" in the 19th century. In 1960s social movements were the ones which aimed at political power within a framework of economic class movements, like labor movements. These movements are named after "old social movements" (Önder, 2003). In these movements, ideological factors were essential for solving out the problematics in the society. The ideology emphasized with fallacies and injustices was required in order to take the action (Hank et al., 1999).

McLuhan was the first communication theorist using the term "global village" in order to emphasize the importance and effect of communication technologies on our daily lives (Aktel, 2001). In other words, this expression paves the way for understanding the inefficiency of geographical borders and the spread of communication tools in order to create a new space for anyone in the world to communicate and be involved in an interaction with the other. The more these tools are spread around the world, the less need people have so as to deal with the issues regarding watching everything from the distance. As mentioned above, the developments of ICTs have quickly made the people go into a change societally as a result of globalization experienced in the last 20 years.

By getting McLuhan's wordings about the world, the term "citizen" becomes the first thing that comes to our minds to redefine with the latest developments and changes. According to Online Cambridge Dictionary, citizen refers to a person who is a member of a particular country and who has rights because of being born there or because of being given rights, or a person who lives in a particular town or city. In the direction of dictionary definition of "citizen" as a word, it suggests a geographic or national definition of social membership. However, it obviously needs to be redefined because communication represents an essential human need as well as a basic human right. As we have seen the rights originating from social membership are involved in the definition of "citizen," it is a must to focus on "netizen" because of communication needs as a human right. As Hauben (1997) stated in the online book titled "Netizens", the word "netizen" reflects the new non-geographically based social membership. In the same book, it is seen

---

1 *abbr.* Information and Communication Technology
2*abbr.* World Wide Web

that two general uses of the term have been developed. The first is a broad usage to refer to anyone who uses the Net, for whatever purpose. The second usage is closer to describe people who care about Usenet and the bigger Net and work toward building the cooperative and collective nature which benefits the larger world (Hauben, 1997). Both uses have been seen recently in different ways because the opportunities found on the Internet changes the way people use it. According to the viewpoint of this chapter, the latter works more in social movements in terms of connectivity via the Internet giving some visible chance to the people-based cooperation and collectivism.

The Internet has affected the communication style and tools among people and the dissemination of information accordingly. The basic change in the era of the Internet is to create another public sphere for the citizens in the cyber world, which is an alternative way for the entire communities all around the world. With the help of globalization, the uses of the Internet weaken the nation states based on participatory democracy and support the awaken of the power of civil command. Many researchers have looked at this new situation optimistic because of a new field opened up and supported by the Internet to give a voice to the people who are out of sight in public. At the very beginning of this new process in 2001, the opponents against the system in Philippines got up using the Internet and removed Estrada with the pressure of mobile technology they made use of (Siegel, 2001). Not only the opponents on any purpose but all disadvantageous groups in silence in the world made themselves heard by using the opportunities of these new technologies.

This chapter seeks to contribute to the worldwide research done scholarly on the use of ICTs by social movements. Specifically, it seeks to explore, analyze and assess the use of social media for LGBTQI mobilization and activities as one of the silent groups mostly in the world, so much the more in Turkey. The several contributions in this chapter present Twitter into the use of spreading the messages and the new form of "activism" in the field of citizen groups and social movements.

## SOCIAL MOVEMENTS IN THE ERA OF WEB 2.0

A social movement includes all who in any form support the general ideas of the movement. Social movements contain social movement organizations, the carrier organizations that consciously attempt to coordinate and mobilize supporters. In the traditional view, social movements are dependent upon their participating members (McCarthy and Zald, 1977). By this definition, social movements make hard work for change in society. These intended changes try to find a way out to be known and to become widespread.

Changes in media commonly-held causes the developments and changes of political propaganda since new. The techniques used for carrying out some propaganda activities are based on the evolving communication tools and practices in order to make the mass society do an act. On the basis of being invisible in the social communication process with the traditional media, these groups of people doing an act for protesting become in need of being active by using new techniques for any purposes. Every social movements try to use any media to disseminate their messages and ideas, but some are not seen in the dominant media fields. Due to this reason, new social movements try to find an opportunity to be visible and active, and also break new ground to make themselves heard. "The Network Society" written by Jan van Dijk in 1999 set out this situation in full. Jan van Dijk stated in the book "A new society model will be shaped and the relations in this society model will be established not face-to-face but through social networks. (Akbıyık and Öztürk, 2012)." That is to say, the society will be shaped organizationally and structurally through social media.

Social media is named as one of the tools used in Web 2.0 which encompasses some changes in the communication environment. The term Web 2.0 was first used in January 1999 by Darcy DiNucci who is an information architecture consultant. DiNucci writes in her article published in the magazine "Fragmented Future" (1999):

> *The Web we know now, which loads into a browser window in essentially static screenfuls, is only an embryo of the Web to come. The first glimmerings of Web 2.0 are beginning to appear, and we are just starting to see how that embryo might develop. The Web will be understood not as screenfuls of text and graphics but as a transport mechanism, the ether through which interactivity happens. It will [...] appear on your computer screen, [...] on your TV set [...] your car dashboard [...] your cell phone [...] hand-held game machines [...] maybe even your microwave oven.*

By getting DiNucci's definition of Web 2.0, we can infer that it focuses on user-generated content, usability and interoperability. Hence, these services allow the people to collaborate and share information online. Rather than the old model where the information is under control, this gives a new paradigm the information seekers control based on the growth of the Internet and their interaction.

These features of characteristics of Web 2.0 are transferred into the social life regarding any kind of movement as three functions: namely, interactivity, collaboration and unions without limits or borders. As Uçkan (2010), who is one of the informal leaders on digital activism in Turkey, said, "Movements on a local scale are paradoxically one of the most effective factors of digital activism and network organization. On the one hand the network effect of digital activism is feeding the opponents by making them interact with global pluralities, on the other hand the effectiveness of local singularities is lifted by globalizing. Especially, protests organized in the cities, even in the districts, lift their effectiveness by creating a tremendous impression on regional, national and international scale. Digital activism spread around the collaborative network created by the people organizing themselves around the topics health, education, transportation, hygiene in the cities and resisting to be alienated with gentrification projects causes critical mass effect by interacting with their counterparts in different countries and/or continents."

In the social movement literature, scholars have suggested an analytical distinction between movements 'changing individual and member behavior versus [those] changing society' (Zald and Ash, 1966). These changes may be experienced in distinctively different ways: in other words, some are based on personal contacts to get any support and the others on searching for the opportunities to change the viewpoint of people living in the same society.

## A SHORT HISTORY OF LGBTQI MOVEMENTS IN TURKEY

Westernization movements has been on the stage since the Republic of Turkey was founded, and developments and changes in almost all cases have been experienced in the society in relation to that. As Karadağ (2008) stated, no official regulations based on positivity or negativity are incident to homosexuality and/or any sexual orientation in the history of the Republic of Turkey. While the fact that there is no negative regulation based on this issue makes possible for the comments on constitutional equality, the fact that both negative and positive regulations are not seen means these identities are not known juridically. That is to say, LGBTQI individuals are left insecure towards negative approaches being faced by them (Karadağ, 2008).

As known internationally, Turkey is a country which is a party to several international agreements protecting the rights of minorities, but not on sexual minorities. According to the current constitution, being homosexual is not illegal. However, this case does not refer to that homosexual individuals have not experienced anything problematic.

The first organizations of sexual minorities are clearly seen in 1990s in order to protect the rights of sexual minorities and to raise the awareness in the society. The first NGO[3] in Turkey was established in 1993 with the name of Lambdaistanbul, and then KaosGL in the year of 1994. In 2005, KaosGL was intended to close down on account of the fact that its charter was unlawful and immoral: however, Ankara Office of Chief Public Prosecutor indicated that there was no reason to close down, and it was not (Karadağ, 2008).

These developments having happened in Turkey refer that sexual minorities have got their rights on being organized, but their positions are still disadvantageous. The most comprehensive study on defining the problems of homosexuals and bisexuals in Turkey was carried out in 2005,

---

3 *abbr.* Non-governmental Organization

and the study consisted of 393 participants with the title "We are neither wrong, not alone – A field research: The problems of homosexuals and bisexuals" by using a questionnaire as the research tool. According to the results of this research, 23% of homosexuals and bisexuals in Turkey are exposed to physical violence, and 87% of them to social violence because of their sexual orientation. 65% and 73% of the participants hide their sexual orientation from their mothers and fathers, respectively. 85% are forced to censor the information regarding their private lives which they would like to share. Most of the participants are faced with discrimination and violence in different organizations they are in, 14% in their educational lives and 18% during their work lives.

Another research titled "Being Us and the Other, Alienation and Discrimination in Turkey: Public Perceptions and Tendencies" was carried out by Hakan Yılmaz in 2010. According to the results based on public opinion survey done with 1811 individuals aged 18 and older, and on in-depth interviews with 40 individuals, Yılmaz (2010) presented that 52% of the participants stated "the rights of sexual minorities living without constraint may be completely limited." In the same research, the question "Who may not express their identities freely?" was answered by 72% with "individuals among sexual minorities like homosexuality."

To see these hidden lives for different reasons, LGBTQI individuals should maintain a positive stance against such discriminations and violence. As stated in a news story published in The New York Times on June 29 in the year of 1969, LGBTQI individuals in Stonewall Inn bar protested against the oppression they had experienced on June 28, 1969. They locked the police exercising influence over them in, clashed four days on the streets and protested. These protests are historically seen as a turning point for LGBTQI rights all around the world, and the subjected days have been celebrated as "Pride Week" in many countries. Pride Week activities have been carried out in Turkey since 2005, and on the last day of the week pride parade was allowedly held until 2016. In 2016 and 2017 the parade to be held on the last day of Pride Week activities was not allowed by the Governorship of Istanbul. In other words, forthcoming experiences about Pride Week cannot be estimated. Usage of social media for Pride Week activities and parade is the basis of this chapter for this very reason.

## THE SITUATION IN PRINTED MEDIA BEFORE LOOKING AT SOCIAL MEDIA[4]

As the studies have changed in time since the 19th century when Richard Freiherr von Krafft-Ebing's book Psychopathia Sexualis, the representation

---

4 This part of the Chapter was summarized with the results from the author's Master Thesis titled with "The Representation of LGBT in Written Media: A Comparative Analysis of Pride Week News in Turkey and the USA" defended at Marmara University's Graduate School of Social Sciences in 2013.

and presence of LGBTQI individuals have also changed in a way that recent developments were done with up-to-date tools. Before screening the social media use by LGBTQI individuals to deal with negative issues they are confronted with and to protest against, to see the historical background of media use is valuable to understand mis- or under-representation culturally. That is to say, the answer of the question on why LGBTQI individuals started using social media to express themselves lies behind their mis-/under-representation or being ignored in traditional media.

In today's world where printed media has fallen from grace and new media technologies have been used to spread the information, the idea that the effect of printed media has disappeared seems relatively wrong. In this sense, a large proportion of the society reach the information via printed media which is a branch of traditional media. Additionally, the differences based on the policy, capital and ideology of any traditional media depict how they want to leave an impression on sensitive angles such as representation. The increase in the dependency of traditional media on information sources is accepted as an evidence of common outputs and discourses becoming widespread.

Considering this idea mentioned in the Master Thesis titled with "The Representation of LGBT Individuals," news stories published in the Pride Week period before 2013 in Turkey were analyzed. Particularly the titles of news stories consist of sentimental referral or leading words, and the content or main body of the news stories does not cover any statistical data and analysis, but just expressions and statements to show the inner messages to the public. Generalization and justification are mostly used with the wordings to represent the LGBTQI individuals who live in Turkey, and the parties involved in the stories become the voice of the messages. The parties change according to the source disseminating the stories regarding LGBTQI individuals and Pride Week.

As mostly disguised words are used to represent this disadvantageous group of individuals by taking rhetoric into consideration, theming is relatively limited. The objectivity of the stories spread in the traditional media shows the imbalance based on the power relations supported by their ideology and/or capital backgrounds. Contradictory discourse is seen even in the news which LGBTQI individuals are the subjects of. Considering LGBTQI individuals in the process of constructing their identities in Turkey, the stories do not consist of many keystones based on the issues they are faced. Therefore, the audience cannot reach the whole information as much as needed to get informed about the topic and are forced to focus on the expression produced with different setbacks. Because of this reason, LGBTQI individuals are seen as just a profile by the public in their social lives. In Turkey, the stories are about a group of individuals whose identities are not mentioned explicitly, who just protest to make an uproar, who are marginalized and commodified as objects of fun.

Shortly, traditional media mostly under-represents LGBTQI individuals in a few senses as they generally do not want to see the reality and show the society as much as they were needed to focus on. In addition to that, LGBTQI individuals intend to find another way to explain themselves, show their presence, show their demands on their needs and be understood fully and scientifically but not with prejudice which does not seem possible to overcome using traditional ways. LGBTQI individuals who are aware of this situation on the Internet having a potential against mainstream media consisting of necessary infrastructure to access and experience the process of Gezi Park protests in Turkey change their ways to the Internet as many other disadvantageous groups of people.

## SOCIAL MEDIA USE IN LGBTQI MOVEMENTS

The Chapter broadly is to determine the contribution of Twitter as a public tool (when compared to the other social media sites) to LGBTQI movements in Turkey by analyzing the accounts of LGBTQI NGOs. To get fell of such contribution to these movements, Pride Week periods were evaluated in this Chapter since 2013 when Gezi Park protests sparked as a keystone politically, socially and culturally in Turkey.

Previous research revealed that mainstream media ignored disadvantageous and/or opponent groups, or reflected them within the status quo. Since this was experienced and understood by those individuals, they quickly started using alternative channels to communicate. As a result of this experience, individuals started using some common things on social media sites to bring their ideas or acts together: for example, with hashtags for Twitter. These items are used mostly to share their point of views, their experiences to deal with, their own contents based on the conditions of the movements for different reasons.

Twitter is a popular social networking and microblogging site where users can post 140-character messages, or tweets. Apart from broadcasting tweets to an audience of followers, Twitter users can interact with one another in two primary public ways: retweets and mentions. Retweets act as a form of endorsement, allowing individuals to rebroadcast content generated by other users, thereby raising the content's visibility (boyd, Golder, and Lotan, 2008). Mentions function differently, allowing someone to address a specific user directly through the public feed, or, to a lesser extent, refer to an individual in the third person (Honeycutt and Herring, 2008). In addition to these two means of communication, hashtags may be used to serve distinct and complementary purposes, together acting as the primary mechanisms for explicit, public user-user interaction on Twitter.

Figure 1: Most Active Social Media Platforms in Turkey

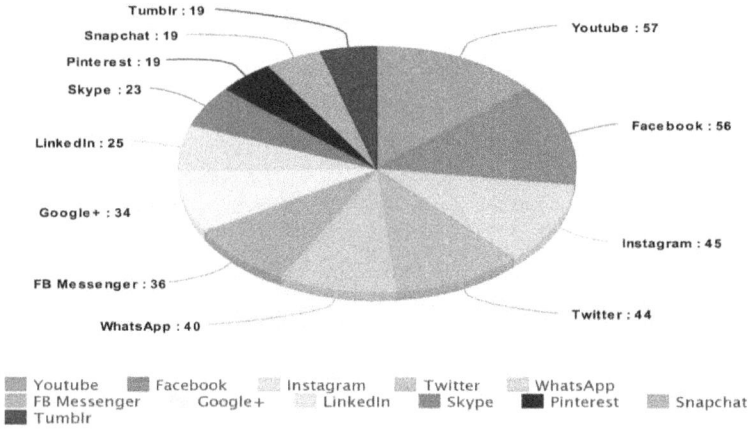

The numbers seen in Figure 1 shows us the user numbers and penetration rates of social media platforms actively used in Turkey, and this makes Twitter as one of the popular subjects for research in several fields of studies. Romero et al. (2010) portrayed influential users, refuting the hypothesis that users with many followers necessarily have bigger impact on the community. With this idea taken into consideration for this Chapter, it can be inferred that hashtags are also important to analyze for understanding the content of LGBTQI NGOs' messages disseminated to the public online. For this reason, screening method was applied on the accounts used by the groups which are national LGBTQI NGOs.

As a result, all the individuals use social media platforms to communicate with each other following the diffusion of the Internet. In this sense, Twitter, as seen in Figure 1, is an essential social media platform to analyze with regard to holding the features of a public sphere by means of hashtags used to spread the words not only by the followers but also even the individuals who are not users. The accounts were double checked to ensure whether the LGBTQI NGOs have used them or not. The ones which cannot be known for certain were opted out for the research.

Social media are computer-mediated technologies that facilitate the creation and sharing of information, ideas, interests and other forms of expression via virtual communities and networks (Obar and Wildman, 2015). Social media are an information sharing sphere where not only professionals, but also common users create content: in other words, not only top-down but also bottom-up (Ozkan, 2014). In this sense, NGOs as ones holding legal entities also need to share content with their audiences, supporters and especially all the people in the sphere of influence. As seen in Table 1, LGBTQI NGOs for their movements, activisms and communication in accordance with national and/or international purposes mostly started making use of Twitter before Gezi Park protests were experienced by the citizens as a keystone based on the events in the history of online and offline activism in Turkey. Accordingly, this situation about when LGBTQI NGOs joined Twitter allows us to see and understand their usage of such social media platforms in terms of change and alteration in their movements.

Table 1: Twitter Accounts of LGBTQI NGOs and Date of Membership

| NGOs | Joined Twitter |
|---|---|
| @KaosGL[5] | October 2009 |
| @lambda_istanbul[6] | April 2010 |
| @siyahpembeucgen[7] | April 2010 |
| @pembehayat_lgbt[8] | October 2010 |
| @istanbulLGBT[9] | April 2011 |
| @hebunlgbt[10] | October 2011 |
| @SPoDLGBTI[11] | November 2011 |
| @KirmiziSemsiyeD[12] | May 2013 |
| @HeviLgbt[13] | July 2013 |
| @genclgbti[14] | December 2016 |

Figure 2 depicts the number of tweets and followers in the accounts of LGBTQI NGOs, and we can infer that @istanbulLGBT is the most penetrated as having the number of followers at most: however, this does not give any background information about whether @istanbulLGBT is able to spread the words with their messages at the very most or not. Since these LGBTQI NGOs in Turkey joined Twitter, each has tweeted variable numbers of content shiftingly based on their frameworks for the sake of their activism areas. The most density since their beginning to use Twitter as a public sphere to share their contents is seen in @KaosGL with 647 tweets per month on an average: following that, 338 tweets by @hebunlgbt, 127

---

5 Kaos Gay and Lesbian Cultural Research and Solidarity Association
6 Lambdaistanbul LGBTI Solidarity Association
7 Black Pink Triangle Izmir Association
8 Pink Life LGBTT Solidarity Association
9 Istanbul LGBTT Solidarity Association
10 Hebûn LGBT Association
11 SPoD LGBT Organization for Equality and Human Rights for Lesbian, Gay, Bisexual and Trans People
12 Red Umbrella Sexual Health and Human Rights Association
13 Hêvî LGBTI Association
14 Youth LGBTI Association

tweets by @HeviLgbt, 87 tweets by @lambda_istanbul, 72 tweets by @istanbulLGBT, 43 tweets by @SPoDLGBTI, 36 tweets by @pembehayat_lgbt, 28 tweets by @genclgbti, 22 tweets by @KirmiziSemsiyeD, and at least 15 tweets by @siyahpembeucgen according to the estimates on a monthly basis when the mean of time spent and output provided on Twitter is calculated.

Figure 2: Tweets and Follower Numbers of LGBTQI NGOs

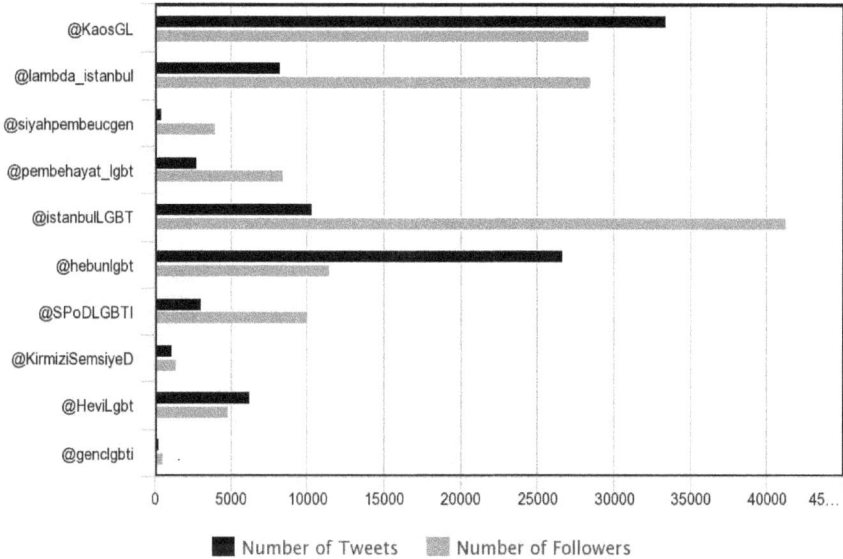

Following the number of tweets and followers, it is obvious that the content created by LGBTQI NGOs holds a considerable influence on spreading the words regarding the issues discussed and experienced by the community. Therefore, looking at the density of content sharing on Twitter in depth paves the way to see the reality based on how the official position of NGOs has changed in years. To find out the position of LGBTQI NGOs on making use of Twitter as a communication tool during Pride Week activities and also Pride Parade, Figure 3 shows the changes in numbers of content shared from the very beginning of even one NGO having joined Twitter. As a consequence, Figure 3 sets the situation starting from 2009 till 2017 when this Chapter was being written.

Until 2013 when Gezi Park protests occurred, LGBTQI NGOs in Turkey did not use Twitter to a large extent. In addition to this, they even did not make use of it in 2013. It is possibly because of the fact that people started expanding their awareness by means of the participation of LGBTQI individuals in Gezi Park protests. Just after that year, the content sharing seemed to boom in different versions Twitter allows: namely, tweets, replies and retweets. In total, 2887 tweets (incl. replies and retweets) were shared during the subjected weeks and when the NGOs made use of Twitter for the purpose of giving themselves a voice on any purposes in Pride Weeks.

Figure 3: Numbers of Tweets, Replies and Retweets during Pride Weeks in Years

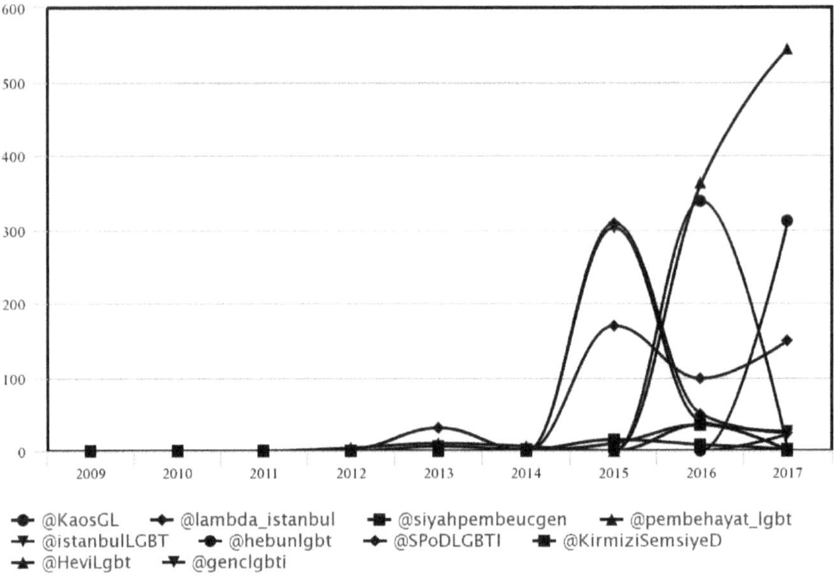

Figure 4: Word Cloud of the Content Shared

Word cloud is a graphic representation of words, typically those used in a document or website, in which the words are arranged artistically in close

proximity and the size of each word's type is proportional to the word's frequency or to the size of a numeric variable associated with the word, such as the population associated with the name of a country[15]. As seen in this word cloud of the hashtags (Figure 4) mostly used by LGBTQI NGOs in Turkey to create their fields of discourse and actuality, the most used hashtag is "#pride" and it is used in English even in Turkish tweets. According to Twitter's Basics Info Page on using Twitter, hashtags allow people to easily follow topics they are interested in. Whence we can understand that LGBTQI NGOs try to spread their words on an international basis to get support against what the individuals are confronted with. The other hashtags[16] mostly used by the NGOs analyzed in this Chapter are "#lgbti, #solidarity, #prideweek, #justiceforahmetyildiz, #lovewins, #sexworkers, #lgbtinpaliament, #myprideismyright, #trans, #civilsocietycannotbesealed, #transpride, #justiceforbuse, #idahot, #onedayonestruggle, #whatisbetweenus #weareparading, #speakupforhandekader." All these hashtags and the related topics discussed in years hold the meaning for equal human rights for any LGBTQI individual. Within the scope of these highlighted topics and/or issues related to LGBTQI individuals in Turkey, it is clearly seen that NGOs make use of Twitter in order to make them known publicly, which is a kind of strategy to become stronger for their activisms. These hashtags holding a message to spread show the LGBTQI movements in Turkey as a part of multi-attribute/-identical struggle.

## CONCLUSION

Today's world and movements evaluated within the scope of globalization and being bounded to the Internet for whatever purposes bring communication technologies into the forefront on the basis of individuals' needs to share. When compared to the movements led in 1960s and 1970s, today's movements are named after digital activism which enables the streets being a public sphere by drawing its strength from the feature "interactivity" of social media platforms. Accordingly, the developments and innovation in technology provide the individuals with an opportunity to reach and spread the information without any borders. This experience creates a non-physical networking area to be organized under the same perspective, share ideas and information without any time and location limits in order to gather the community members together.

As seen in the historical and contemporary trends of movements, social media platforms, namely Twitter in this Chapter, enable LGBTQI individuals in Turkey create a huge effect on people by spreading their contents nationally or internationally. This case is clearly seen with the

---

15 word cloud. (n.d.) American Heritage® Dictionary of the English Language, Fifth Edition. (2011). Retrieved September 7 2017 from http://www.thefreedictionary.com/word+cloud

16 The hashtags used in Turkish were translated into English.

numbers of the followers, tweets and their density during the most essential periods, such as Pride Weeks. According to the content constructed by LGBTQI NGOs on Twitter, the LGBTQI individuals have been still trying to express themselves for different reasons such as being seen as the ones who are unhealthy, have disorderly behaviors, are oppressed because of their sexual orientations and are faced with the violation of human rights.

As a consequence, communication technologies and online platforms power LGBTQI individuals up because they may not be excluded under favor of the fact that ICTs expanding the scope of freedom of expression and providing an opportunity to represent themselves properly. As seen in the contents and the numbers reflecting that LGBTQI NGOs started making use of Twitter, social media use in any kind of movements is an epiphany of normality in this era.

## REFERENCES

Akbıyık, N. & Öztürk, M. (2012) "Sivil Toplum ve Sosyal Medya Perspektifinde 'Arap Baharı' ve 'Wall Strett'i İşgal Et' Eylemleri", *Turgut Özal Uluslararası Ekonomi ve Siyaset Kongresi II*, pp. 1003 – 1027.

Aktel, M. (2001) "Küreselleşme Süreci ve Etki Alanları", Süleyman Demirel Üniversitesi İdari ve İktisadi Bilimler Fakültesi Yayını, 6.

Boyd, D., Golder, S. & Lotan, G. (2008) "Tweet, tweet, retweet: Conversational aspects of retweeting on twitter", *Hawaii International Conference on Systems Sciences*.

DiNucci, D. (1999) "Fragmented Future" (PDF). Print 53 (4).

Hank, J. et al. (1999) "Kimlikler, Sikayetler ve Yeni Sosyal Hareketler", *Yeni Sosyal Hareketler*, İstanbul: Kaknüs.

Hajnal, P. I. (2002) "Civil society in the information age" England: Ashgate.

Hauben, M., & Hauben, R. (1997) "Netizens: on the history and impact of usenet and the Internet." Los Alamitos, CA: IEEE Computer Society.

Honeycutt, C. & Herring, S. C. (2008) "Beyond microblogging: Conversation and collaboration via Twitter", *Hawaii International Conference on Systems Sciences*.

Karadağ, N. (2008) *Cinsel Azınlıkların Bireysel Hakları*, İstanbul: XII Levha Yayınları.

McCarthy, J. D. & Zald, M. N. (1977) "The trend of social movements in America: Professionalization and resource mobilization."

Obar, J A. & Wildman, S. (2015) "Social media definition and the governance challenge: An introduction to the special issue", *Telecommunications policy*. 39 (9), 745-750.

Önder, T. (2003) "Ekoloji, Toplum ve Siyaset", Ankara: Odak.

Özkan, Ö. (2014) "Sosyal Medya ve Kültürel Değerler", *I Uluslararası Yeni Medya Yeni Yaklaşımlar Konferansı*.

Romero, D. M., Galuba, W., Asur, S. & Huberman, B. A. (2010) "Influence and Passivity in Social Media", Technical Report.

Siegel, J. (2001) "Philippine citizens overthrow President Joseph Estrada", People Power II.

Uçkan, Ö. (2010) "Dijital aktivizm ne kadar etkili?", Gennaration, (Vol 5.)

Yılmaz, H. (2010) "Biz"lik, "Öteki"lik, Ötekilşetirme ve Ayrımcılık: Kamuoyundaki Algılar ve Eğilimler, Bihai İçeriksel Rapor, Açık Toplum Vakfı, İstanbul.

Zald, M. N. & Ash, R. (1966) "Social movement organizations: growth, decay and change", Social Forces (Vol. 44)

# PART II

# CONTEXTUAL ANALYSIS

.

# CHAPTER 6

## QUEER CHARACTERS AND GENDER PERFORMANCES IN SAIT FAIK'S WORKS

### Nazan Maksudyan

As Talat Sait Halman notes, Sait Faik (1906 – 1954) was the master of the short story in Turkish literature. He wrote almost two hundred stories, two novellas, a number of essays, and nearly forty poems. He is mostly known for his realistic short stories, dwelling upon fishermen, workers, children, beggars, wanderers in some neighborhoods in the city of Istanbul. He is also exceptional in giving voice to the non-Muslim communities in the city in the 1930s and 1940s. His literary genius rested on the fact that he "portrayed the predicaments, maladjustments, and disillusionments of the man in the street, frequently himself, living on the fringes of the society."[1]

Sait Faik represents a milestone in Turkish literature in the sense that he has broadened the possible cast of characters by including people who were so far excluded.[2] He wrote about the poor people, workers, the homeless, thieves, criminals, lunatics, people with disabilities and illnesses, drug users, prostitutes, displaced people, flâneurs, and non-Muslims. Within his general cast made up of the "underdog", there were not only the poor, the underclass, the non-Muslims, the immigrants, but also those who were sexually marginalized and the queer. Biographical and literary works on Sait Faik very briefly touch upon his gay sexual orientation and the homoerotic nature of his works. The hidden sexual content of his work has previously been mentioned, albeit not in a detailed manner, by a number of literary critics.[3] However, leaving aside a discussion of biographical truth to his sexuality, it can easily be argued that he was the first great writer of fiction to

---

1 Talat Sait Halman, "Preface", in *Sleeping in the Forest: Stories and Poems* (Syracuse: Syracuse University Press, 2004), vii.

2 Süha Oğuzertem, "Introduction: Sait Faik's Utopian Poetics and the Lyrical Turn in Turkish Fiction", in *Sleeping in the Forest: Stories and Poems* (Syracuse: Syracuse University Press, 2004), xv.

3 Fethi Naci, *Sait Faik'in Hikâyeciliği* (Istanbul: Yapı Kredi Yayınları, 2003); Oğuz Cebeci, *Psikanalitik Edebiyat Kuramı* (Istanbul: İthaki Yayınları, 2004); Yıldırım Türker, "Bir Serüven," *Kaos GL* 102 (2008): 14; Murat Belge, "Eşcinsellik," in *Edebiyat Üstüne Yazılar* (Istanbul: İletişim Yayınları, 1998), 446-52.

include queer gender performances into his mix of characters.[4]

Reference guides to literary representations of homosexual love are numerous.[5] Meyers notes that the clandestine predilections of homoerotic love are both an obstacle and a stimulus to art, and lead to a creative tension between repression and expression.[6] The authors needed to find a language of reticence and evasion, obliqueness and indirection, to convey their theme. The expression of homoerotic love in the early twentieth century had to be subtle, allusive, and symbolic. As the author was trying to express a repressed, hidden, and essentially a secret theme, the narrative and expression was ambiguous. The cautious and covert qualities of the language enforced concealment instead of revealing. These were the dilemmas of Sait Faik, trying to publicly express feelings and acts, that are both considered taboo, sin, or even crimes. Societal taboos reinforced intolerance and rejection. His works had the qualities of subtlety, ambiguity, elusiveness, and restraint that define the likes of its genre.

The constant anxiety, fear, and sense of "being caught" intensified isolation and introspection. As Eve Kosofsky Sedgwick clearly delineates in her study, *Epistemology of the Closet*, being "closeted", being hidden away in a dark closet, was also the literary style used to describe homoerotic intimacy.[7]

In this chapter, I aim to approach the literature of Sait Faik from the perspective of gender performances and the queer theory. Queer theory's emphasis on a politics of difference and marginality and its critique of heterosexual hegemony and patriarchy are important inspirations for the expression of sexual plurality and gender ambivalence.[8] Sait Faik's work is remarkable in its inclusionary attitude towards different sorts of marginality. He had always defended the fundamental human equality and his radical humanitarianism had encompassed his writings. This inclusive and democratic perspective made it possible for him to discuss different sexual *disorientations*[9], male homosocialities, gay and lesbian eroticism and sexualities, and queer performances. His works are exceptional in portraying gender performances that challenge the dominant gender regime and the existential crisis of queer characters. Moreover, his characters question orthodoxies and

---

4 I have learned a lot and benefitted greatly from the analysis of Oğuz Güven, "Sait Faik'in Hikaye ve Romanlarında Homoerotizm, Erkek İmgesi Kadın Temsilleri," unpublished MA thesis (Bilkent University, 2010).

5 Wayne R. Dynes and Stephen Donaldson (eds.), *Homosexual Themes in Literary Studies* (New York: Garland, 1992); Stuart Kellogg (ed.), *Literary Visions of Homosexuality* (New York: Haworth, 1983), Sharon Malinowski and Christa Brelin, *The Gay and Lesbian Literary Heritage: A Reader's Companion to the Writers and Their Works, from Antiquity to the Present* (New York: Holt, 1995); Gregory Woods, *A History of Gay Literature: The Male Tradition* (New Haven: Yale University Press, 1998).

6 Jeffrey Meyers, *Homosexuality and Literature, 1890-1930* (London: Athlone Press, 1977), 1.

7 Eve Kosofsky Sedgwick, *Epistemology of the Closet* (Berkeley: University of California Press, 1990), 3.

8 Raman Selden, Peter Widdowson, Peter Brooker, *A Reader's Guide to Contemporary Literary Theory* (Harlow: Pearson Longman, 2005), 253.

9 I use the word "disorientation" instead of the common expression "orientation", to challenge the essentialism in an orientation.

promote or provoke gender uncertainties, that force the read beyond heterosexual, lesbian and gay sexualities and to imagine a range of other sexualities that challenge such fixed or settled categorizations.

## SEXUAL DISORIENTATION

Queer theory refuses an essentialist reading of gender identities and emphasizes the constructedness, ambivalence and potential plurality of all gendered and sexual identities. As Halperin notes, the queer is an identity without an essence, "there is nothing in particular to which it necessarily refers", except from the fact it is always at odds with the "normal".[10]

It is necessary to underline that the beginning of the twentieth century in Turkey, and also elsewhere in the world, was not a time of openness and freedom regarding one's sexual imaginaries and tendencies. While analyzing the literature of Sait Faik from the perspective of sexual *disorientation*, the issue of self-censorship becomes important. Literary analyses on late nineteenth and early twentieth century homosexual writings have underlined this form of restraint, leading even to a literary style, marked by subtle indirectness, the use of coded statements, and the portrayal of passionate devotion instead of the sexual act.[11] Sedgwick notes that "closetedness" itself is a performance initiated as such by the speech act of a silence.[12] In that respect, "silence is rendered as pointed and performative as speech, in relations around the closet" and "ignorance is as potent and as multiple" as knowledge.[13] The isolation, in return, heightens the intellectual defiance of the social outcast who is forced to question and challenge conventional ideas about morality and art.

Ahmet Oktay notes that neither the legal structure nor social conditions were appropriate for Sait Faik to articulate in a clear manner on his sexual disorientation.[14] Moreover, the Turkish literary tradition did not yet have such works, professing confessions of this sort. This is why queer sexuality in his works were described under a curtain or a mask, which, on the other hand, implicitly confirmed their very existence.[15] Still, several of his short stories and novels manages to "disorient" the sexual normality and question

---

10 David M. Halperin, One Hundred Years of Homosexuality and Other Essays on Greek Love (London: Routledge, 1990).

11 Wayne R Dynes, Stephen Donaldson, *Homosexual Themes in Literary Studies* (New York: Garland, 1992), 8.

12 Eve Kosofsky Sedgwick, *Epistemology of the Closet* (Berkeley: University of California Press, 1990), 3.

13 Ibid., 4.

14 The existence and commonality of male homosexuality in the Ottoman Empire, especially prior to nineteenth century, has been stressed as an important factor in the performance and persistence of queer identities in the modern period. Donna Landry, "Queering Identities in Ottoman History and Turkish Identity", in *Turkey and the Politics of National Identity: Social, Economic and Cultural Transformation*, Shane Brennan, Marc Herzog (eds.) (New York : I.B. Tauris, 2014), 215-243.

15 Ahmet Oktay, "Kabul ve Red: Yalnızlığın Kutupları," in *Kabul ve Red* (Istanbul: Simavi Yayınları, 1992), 83-98.

essentializing tendencies and binary thinking in sexuality.

In his analysis of the short stories of Sait Faik, Fethi Naci noted that in the famous four stories in *Alemdağ'da Var Bir Yılan* and few others that followed them, Sait Faik broke away from his fears and started to write more openly about his sexual orientation. Naci notes that once he exercised a certain degree of freedom of writing, he wrote with unprecedented courage, daring to express his orientation almost clearly without considering criticisms.[16] Naci underlines that, those orientations that remained hidden or latent until now, became the most important things to write about for him. It is reminiscent of his famous sentence at the end of "A Dot on the Map": "I would go mad if I hadn't write." Sait Faik had to write about this love affair between two men.

"A Story Just like that" ("Öyle Bir Hikâye"), "Human Created by Loneliness" ("Yalnızlığın Yarattığı İnsan") ve "There is a Snake in Alemdağı ("Alemdağı'nda Var Bir Yılan"), and "The Dream of Panco" ("Panco'nun Rüyası") in *Alemdağ'da Var Bir Yılan* (1954) are mostly about İshak, looking for his lover whom he has lost, submerged in a feeling of great loneliness. İshak walks in the dark streets of Istanbul at night, thinks of Panco, confesses his love for him, and speaks to him in dreamlike conversations. İshak's existential crisis and "melancholy" is very similar to what Butler notes in *The Psychic Life of Power*. She underlines that exclusionary prohibitions determined by the hegemonic social order, upon homosexuality for example, results in a melancholy loss of what is forbidden but cannot be avowed.[17] As the existence of a love affair between the two men becomes hard to deny, the text also gets more complex and difficult to follow. All written in the 1950s, these stories had a great degree of discreetness, which led to some literary analysts to interpret them as Sait Faik's flirtation with surrealism. The affair of İshak and Panco was buried deep within a quite fragmented text, having confusing slips of time and space in the narrative. However, when analyzing literature through queer theory, gray area between author and reader, male and female, light and dark, good and evil are all enmeshed. A new set of critical eyes can see the completely different subtext to these short stories.[18] The characters that we think we know so well become newly strange, and a whole set of new questions arise. The issue of sexuality in these stories, therefore, is discernible through a critical reading.

İshak feels suffocated with loneliness, as he cannot find Panco. In one of the very well known quotes of his literature, he says, "loneliness has filled the world" (Yalnızlık dünyayı doldurmuş) (25). Yet, the loneliness that he is

---

16 Fethi Naci, Sait Faik'in Hikâyeciliği, 56.

17 Judith Butler, *The Psychic Life of Power: Theories in Subjection* (California: Stanford University Press, 1997).

18 For a discussion on queer theory and its impact on literary criticism, see Judith Butler, *Gender Trouble: Feminism and the Subversion of Identity* (New York: Routledge, 1992) and Eve Kosofsky Sedgwick, *Between Men: English Literature and Male Homosocial Desire* (New York: Columbia University Press, 1985).

speaking of is not a momentary or a temporary one. It is not solely about losing Panco. Certain passages make it clear that he is talking about an eternal loneliness, imposed by the heteronormative structure of the society. He realizes that he and his lover are not allowed to be a couple, they are not allowed to act as a couple in this societal, moral, and/or religious order. They are bound to be alone, or else with a woman.

> *"I would go again to that beer-house in that passage. At that table I would sit, at that table. People would come and sit, all in couples, men and women. Me, on my own. In millions, on my own. The pain hurts more and more. A pain like bitter melon, like poison. The thing we find after we lose. Guess what? Guess what?" (18)[19]*

These words make it clear that he suffers not only from loneliness, but also from the societal pressure upon his sexual disorientation. As heterosexuality is the norm in the society, the relationship of two men cannot be lived publicly. It had to be hidden, it had to be a secret, it had to be lived alone. İshak remembers two instances where Panco tried to hide himself so as not to be seen together with him. In the first one, he hides behind someone in a bar and in the other one he passes by him "as if passing by a wall or a dead cat" (26).[20] As the city and the crowds constantly threaten gay intimacies, İshak dreams of going to more suburban neighborhoods such as Alemdağ, where no one knows them and where they have a little room to take shelter. But there came a moment in İshak's life where he feels no longer easy about this secrecy and loneliness. The following words convey an essential disaccord with the society and an opposition to the social values: "I was on the streets. I was one against thousands. I was one against ten thousands." (18)[21]

His sexuality made him feel like a social outcast, a marginal; he was no longer a part of the majority. Therefore, he felt not only threatened and excluded, but also felt empowered as a rebel, as a lonely warrior. He talks to a stray dog and gives him some good news regarding the future. He reveals to him that we, humans, would soon have an entirely new morality, a new way of seeing and interpreting things that will change Panco's mind and take away his religious fears as well.

> *"We will have a morality that no book has ever written. A morality, that will look in amazement at what we do today, what we will do, in what we think, in what we will think (...) And then, my friend Panco will also agree with me, he will not speak of the church morality. He will tell his children about the extraordinary beauty of friendship."*

---

19 "O pasajdaki birahaneye yine gitsem. O masaya otursam o masaya. İnsanlar gelse otursa çift çift kadınlı erkekli. Ben tek başıma. Milyonlar içinde tek başıma. Acı gitgide acıyor. Kavun acısı gibi, zehir gibi bir acı. Kaybettikten sonra bulduğumuz şey."

20 "Bir duvarın, ölmüş bir kedinin yanından geçer gibi."

21 "Caddelerdeydim. Binlere karşı birdim. On binlere karşı birdim."

*(8-9)[22]*

Despite the implicit nature of the language, the dream of İshak is apparently a new world order, where male homoeroticism and queer love is not considered to be a sin, a perversion, or a crime. He assumes that Panco would be a father, a typical family guy, but still he would acknowledge the beauty and value of what they had with İshak. These four stories about İshak and Panco, in *Alemdağ'da Var Bir Yılan*, underlines the impossibilities ahead of two men to be together, especially because of the fears and feelings of guilt caused by internalized bourgeois notions of a rigid, patriarchal heterosexuality. However, retrospectively speaking, he is making a valid guess that there would come a time in human history, when heteronormative structure of the society would be shattered and the gender regime would include the queer. Sait Faik, therefore, imagines the realization of an elusive sexuality, fragmented into local, *deviant*, and *perverse* particularities (such as pederastic and voyeuristic desires that he has written at length about).[23]

## MALE HOMOSOCIALITIES AND GAY EROTICISM

Sait Faik wrote to a large extent short stories about men, with predominantly male characters. In author's short stories and novels, the reader hear the voices of men from different age groups, be it boys, teenagers, adults, or old men. His stories are frequently set in typical gendered male spaces that construct the essence of male homosocial culture in Turkey, such as coffee shops, taverns and barbershops.[24] Sedgwick deploys the concept of "homosociality" as an interpretative tool to understand different historical shapes, articulations and mechanisms of inequality in both male and female spaces.[25] Sait Faik also focused on certain male activities that exclude women, such as fishing. Such spaces and activities, where male characters co-exist, where they earn money or chat with other men, have allowed Sait Faik to focus more on men's experiences, thus leaving a smaller space for women in the narrative.

Sait Faik's literature has been analyzed for the extent of homoeroticism in it and also for possible clues for the author's own sexual orientation. Several literary analyses make it clear that the author, at least in more than a dozen short stories, described gay relationships, or else homoerotic male

---

22 "Bir ahlakımız olacak ki hiçbir kitap daha yazmadı. Bir ahlakımız, bugün yaptıklarımıza, yapacaklarımıza, düşündüklerimize, düşüneceklerimize hayretler içinde bakan bir ahlakımız. [….] O zaman hiç merak etme. Dostum Panco da bana hak verecektir. Kilise ahlakından söz açmayacak. Dostluğun olağanüstü güzelliğini çocuklarına anlatacak."

23 Oğuz Güven analyzes in detail the pederastic content in Sait Faik's short stories. Oğuz Güven, "Sait Faik'in Hikaye ve Romanlarında Homoerotizm, Erkek İmgesi Kadın Temsilleri," unpublished MA thesis (Bilkent University, 2010), 46-48.

24 Hülya Arık, "Kahvehanede Erkek Olmak: Kamusal Alanda Erkek Egemenliğin Antropolojisi," in *Cins Cins Mekân*, Ayten Alkan (ed.) (Istanbul: Varlık Yayınları, 2009), 168-201.

25 Eve Kosofsky Sedgwick, *Between Men, English Literature and Male Homosocial Desire* (New York: Columbia University Press, 1985).

desire. His homoerotic texts often build upon the feelings, impressions and associations of usually a middle-aged man, who is attracted to quite young boys from lower social classes.[26] All homoerotic texts of Sait Faik are also stories of unhappiness in which the experience of homosexuality is obstructed, remain broken, and thus impossible. Almost all of these short stories are written with a quite covert language. Some of them, like "Louvre'dan Çaldığım Heykel" (The sculpture I stole from Louvre), take a fantastic turn as the author does not dare to elaborate on his actual sentiments and desires.

Halman states that there are a few gay characters and actions in some of Sait Faik's stories. These are only rarely written in a manifest manner. Otherwise, they are put in extremely secret words and settings. Sait Faik benefits from the gender neutral nature of the Turkish language. An enabling feature of Turkish as a language for a plurality of sexual identifications and affects, one of its openings to queerness in all its multiplicity, is its lack of gendering. The third person singular pronoun is simply 'O'. O can be male, female, queer, an animal, or even a thing.[27] Andrews and Kalpaklı underline the value of this ambiguity as a valuable androgyny, as a challenge to the binary sexualities, and as a blurring of the fixed gendering itself. Therefore, it becomes an even more valuable indeterminacy.[28] Therefore, in some stories of Sait Faik, it is impossible to tell the gender of the protagonist and his/her loved one.

"Fear of Love" is such a story, where the characters do not have names, so as to make the reader imagine the described intimacy. The homosexual content in this story is extremely hidden. This blurred narrative character, full of uncertainties, avoids telling the name of the lover and also other possible depictions that could reveal his/her gender. The narrative is also silent about the name of the small mountain town that the short story is set. However, since it is a part of the subsection "Those who returned from a journey with me", it is possible to assume that this was a European city. The narrator, possibly an adult male, spends time in the empty and partially dark streets of this mountain town. He goes to a working class neighborhood, away from the city center, meets his lover in a movie theater. They watch a film hand in hand and then they go to his dark and empty room without saying a word to each other. The centrality of darkness and anonymity in the short story is remarkable. The city streets are dark, the movie theater is naturally dark, and the room of the narrator is dark. There are no names and there is no spoken word between the characters. All these suggest that the so-called lovers probably did not even know each other. Maybe they have

---

26 Pederastic desire in gay literature has been a largely discussed topic. Patrick Pollard, *André Gide: Homosexual Moralist* (London: Yale University Press, 1991).

27 Donna Landry, "Queering Identities in Ottoman History and Turkish Identity", 221.

28 Walter G. Andrews, Mehmet Kalpaklı, The Age of Beloveds: Love and the Beloved in Early-Modern Ottoman and European Culture and Society (Durham: Duke University Press, 2005).

just found each other in the theater and then left together. In any case, this is a secret relationship, lived in secluded places and far away from the crowds. It is, therefore, not a public or a socially sanctioned affair.

The unapproved nature of the relationship is also obvious from the described feelings of guilt of the narrator. He says, "after he left, I, as devastated as if I killed him, I would wait for the morning, the police, the law, on my murderer bed." (77) Based on these words, the reader gets the feeling that the narrator had done something bad. There is rarely any physical intimacy described in any of Sait Faik's short stories, except for a few innocent kisses and hugs. The example above is a vague suggestion that the couple had experienced a form of closeness. Yet, the narrator is so unused to the act itself that he feels quite devastated and cannot handle his own loneliness, nakedness, and idleness when the lover is no longer next to him. Fethi Naci argues that the guilt was resulting from the fear of dragging another person to one's own hell. Therefore, the narrator had this "fear of love", because his love makes him unhappy and there is the risk that he is making somebody else also unhappy.

> *"I am afraid to love. I know that it is a lonely thing, which will leave me idle and completely naked, a vagrant in every possible sense of the word; and I am scared of it as I fear the dark, hypocrisy, cruelty, unfreedom." (75)*[29]

"Battaniye" (Blanket), published posthumously in 1954, similar to the "Fear of Love", also leaves the gender of the lover in the short story uncertain. There are barely any descriptive passages in the story that help the reader to imagine the physical characteristics of this lover. "Blanket" only touches upon the "curly hair", "clever eyes" and the age (around twenties) of this person lying carelessly on the narrator's bed, on a blanket and glancing through magazines. It is clear from a number of sentences that he is a paid lover, he comes to the apartment of the narrator because of some sort of financial compensation. This is why the narrator is in constant doubt about whether he is doing something bad or not, whether bad things bring about good things, whether their relationship is based on love or not. Despite his never-ending doubts and nightmares, he cannot help but think:

> *"Regardless of the reasons that brought him [onu] to me, this magnificent result is right here, on the blanket, immersed into the pictorial, the result that will unleash me to new friendships, loves, the twenties [as in age], health and happiness, friendship and inner piece. What else do I want?" (367)*[30]

The story leaves quite a distance between the two lovers in the sense that

---

29 "Sevmekten korkuyorum. Başka arzular, ihtiraslarla atıldığım yolda beni avare ve çırılçıplak, başı her manada boş bırakacak yalnız bir şey olduğunu biliyorum ve ondan karanlıktan, riyadan, zulümden, hürriyetsizlikten korkar gibi ürküyorum."

30 "Onu bana getiren sebepler ne olursa olsun bu battaniyenin üstündeki resimli dergiye dalmış harikulade netice, beni dostluklara, sevdalara, yirmi yaşlara, sıhhatlere ve saadetlere, arkadaşlıklara ve huzurlara salan netice karşımda işte. Daha ne isterim."

there is no dialogue between them and the young and attractive one is depicted constantly as lying down, while the older narrator is potentially standing and watching his *trophy*. He even admits that what he only wants is to watch him sleep on this blanket once a week. In his "Fiction of a Flâneur", Halman states that Sait Faik's protagonist is always a flâneur and a voyeur.[31] The act of watching, observing other people had a desirable, even sexual value for him. Watching a loved male friend sleep appears as a recurrent theme in a number of short stories[32] and it is clear that the act of the voyeur is a substitute for sexual intercourse.

## QUEER PERFORMANCES

In "Gender as Performance" (1994), Judith Butler rejects the essentialism of hetero/homosexual binary opposition and suggests the queering of heterosexist narratives.[33] From that perspective, queer theory calls for a disruption of normative sexual identities and an understanding of agency that is linked to the performance of those identities. Butler's idea of performativity with sexual or gendered identities suggests the existence of a theatrical self, free to choose from a range of possible stylized acts. The self in this configuration becomes performative, improvisational, and discontinuous.[34]

In Sait Faik's short stories, many male and female characters break the stereotypical gender performativity and can best be defined as queer characters. These characters are queer with their appearances, their behavior in society, their roles in their relationships.[35] It is especially worth noting that Sait Faik's characters challenge the established gender roles and gender regime imposed by the society. His several female characters openly oppose the gender stereotypes. They are portrayed in settings that are considered exclusively for male performances, such as traditional cafes (*kahvehane*), taverns (*meyhane*) and barbershops. In this section, I will discuss a number of queer characters that portray the genius of Sait Faik in creating a world of gender performances.

In "Eleni and Katina" (1944), in *Havada Bulut* (Cloud in the Sky) narrator Ahmet Bey, describes the nineteen-year-old Katina and her love affair with Eleni. He says, "the most curious thing was Katina's love. Although she met every night with me or with another man, or sometimes with his boss, Katina

---

31 Talat Sait Halman, "Introduction: Fiction of a Flâneur," in *A Dot On The Map: Selected Stories And Poems* (Bloomington: Indiana University Turkish Studies, 1995), 3-11.

32 "Kaşıkadası'nda", "Yalnızlığın Yarattığı İnsan", "Battaniye".

33 Peter Osborne and Lynne Segal, "Gender as Performance: An Interview with Judith Butler,", *Radical Philosophy* 67 (1994): 32-39.

34 Moe Meyer (ed.), *The Politics and Poetics of Camp* (New York: Routledge, 1994).

35 For a very detailed analysis of queer culture in Turkey, see Cüneyt Çakırlar, Serkan Delice (eds.), *Cinsellik Muamması: Türkiye'de Queer Kültür ve Muhalefet* (Istanbul: Metis, 2012).

was not in love with none of us, but a young girl." (83)[36] After learning that she was in love with a girl, Ahmet Bey's interest in Katina increases. He says, there has been a strange change in how he feels about Katina, that he wanted to see her more often. They "never talk about her habit" (bu huyundan hiç bahsetmezdik), but now Ahmet Bey "was seeing her differently" (onu şimdi başka türlü görürdüm). These few lines suggest a genuine interest on the part of Ahmet Bey, not imbued by typical male phantasies or societal judgment. He simply wants to spend more time with this different woman, as other characters in other Sait Faik stories wants to spend more time with poor fishermen or beggar children.

One night, he sees her with her lover, Eleni. In this encounter Katina was unusual, she was "carefree, light-hearted, in touch with the world". She smiles at Ahmet Bey "like a man" and shakes his hand "mightily". The narrative draws particular attention to non-feminine traits of Katina to strengthen her queerness. As he looks after them, he feels full of hope and happiness for their love and bright future. These words make it clear that the narrator was impressed by the love he witnessed and he was definitely not judgmental regarding this queer form of love.

*"When they left looking contented, I looked after them. The long and slender legs of Katina's friend and a little thicker, naked (çorapsız), white legs of Katina seemed to run towards laughter and fun, to a clean world, that is far away from poverty and misery." (83)[37]*

What is worth emphasizing about "Eleni and Katina" is that, Sait Faik had written this short story on female homosexuality quite frankly, unlike his stories on male homosexuality, which are rather concealed with uncertainties and other narrative techniques. The author wrote about male homosexuality in a very subtle way, these texts even took him closer to fantastic and surreal literature. "Eleni and Katina", on the other hand, openly and proudly presents the love of two women.

The hairdresser Rıza in "Bayan Gülseren" is portrayed as a typical queer character. The two nicknames that were given to him, "the beautiful coiffure" (berber güzeli) and "Jules" (Jül), both had gay connotations. The physical features of him were also described as defying the male gender performances. He had a very thin mustache, making him feminine (kadınsılaştırmak) and he was having his eyebrows plucked (kaşlarını da almış). This was a practice, traditionally reserved to women and a man performing it suggested nothing but a queer performance. Gülseren, sitting as a customer in front of him, was criticizing all these feminine characteristics in her mind

---

36 "İşin en tuhafı, Katina'nın aşkıydı. Her akşam benimle yahut başka bir adamla, bazen patronuyla buluşmasına rağmen Katina, bizim üçümüze de değil, bir genç kıza âşıktı."

37 "Benden mesut ayrılırlarken arkalarından baktım. Katina'nın dostunun ince uzun bacaklarıyla Katina'nın biraz kalınca, çorapsız, beyaz bacakları gülmeye, eğlenmeye, fakirlikten ve sefaletten uzak, temiz bir dünyaya doğru koşar gibiydiler."

and imagining to guide him to change these habits. Sait Faik's analysis of queer performances and how they were typically perceived by the society is quite delicate and nuanced. Rıza, the gay hairdresser, is an eternal and a timeless character. He is a closeted homosexual, trying to partially express his identity through little gestures of beauty. Yet, he is generally observed by the society as a wrong performer. Many contemporaries of Zeki Müren, for instance, a flamboyant though never explicitly declared queer, claimed that they never used to "think of him as gay." It is true that "queer" was not a public and labeled social category in the 1950s and 1960s in Turkey. There were, however, many ways in which queerness was publicly performed and negotiated at the time.[38]

Sait Faik also rightly noted that the fact that queer male character is observed as an object of desire is also a typical societal response to differing performances of gender. Rıza was actually considered to be beautiful, as his nickname suggests. Gülseren was also truly attracted to him. In that respect, Rıza was assumed to be a heterosexual man, who is therefore potentially available for an affair with a woman (Gülseren), despite some minor "retouches" she had in mind. The imaginary attempts of Gülseren to "correct" him into true masculinity are typical of the heteronormative gender regime.

Another queer character that is worth noting is a 14-year-old girl in "Medar-ı Maişet Motoru" (1944) which was later published as *Birtakım İnsanlar*. Melek appears as one of the leading characters in this novella, as a female next to four boys. Unlike typical teenage female beauty descriptions that are very frequent in Turkish literature, Sait Faik describes a tomboy. Melek had very big hands and feet, broad shoulders, and a flat chest (*göğsü düz, yayvan*). The girl did not only have a masculine body, she also frequented with a bunch of boys, as a member of a gang. Her professional career also takes a strange turn, when her father insists that she works as an apprentice of a male barber, Dimitro. Melek's original idea was to be a tailor, but her father, Ali Riza was thrilled to think that he would be the father of the first Turkish barber girl. Given the sexual division of labor in the 1930s, there are a number challenges to the gender regime. First, it is unusual for a male master to have a female apprentice. Furthermore, it is very unlikely for a girl to open a barbershop of her own, since these are typical places of male sociability excluding the presence of women.[39] Still, Sait Faik reflects upon

---

38 For a general analysis of how the Turkish society has dealt with queer identities on the level of popular culture, a discussion of Zeki Müren might be enlightening. Martin Stokes notes that the responses to Müren's queerness have been ambivalent. There was on the one hand the "fear of the effeminate man", but many simply chose to ignore this aspect of Müren's personality. Yet relatively few people objected publicly, and in the years following his death the theme of his queerness emerged as an explicit topic of public conversation. Martin Stokes, *The Republic of Love: Cultural Intimacy in Turkish Popular Music* (Chicago: University of Chicago Press, 2010), 36.

39 Beauty industry became a female profession only after the 1980s in Turkey. Before that hairdressing was a predominantly male occupation. Claudia Liebelt, "Grooming Istanbul: Intimate

the "motherly character" of Dimitro, as yet another twist in the possible range of gender performances.

Nevin, in *Kayıp Aranıyor* (1953), is also an extraordinary female character who disregards the behavior patterns that are expected of women in the dominant gender regime. The novel is a fragmented account of Nevin's relationships with three different men and her recollections of searching for happiness. In the narrative, identity, transvestism, contradictory sexuality, search for individual morality, eroticism and violence come to the forefront. Nevin can be regarded as one of the most complex female characters of Turkish literature with her ideas, emotional relationships, and conflicts. Nevin is a twenty-five-year-old intellectual woman, who studied abroad, knows a few foreign languages, and works as a journalist and a translator. She is the daughter of the retired consul. *Kayıp Aranıyor* recounts a series of events that Nevin lived through in 1947-48. The novel starts with her divorce from her husband, who is also a journalist and her short love affair with a fisherman.

In a flashback, she remembers a day and a discussion with her husband in Ankara. Then, the narrator intervenes to comment on the specialty of Nevin. In this section, the narrator describes some intimate friendships that Nevin had with other men in the small town (Beykoz). Since Nevin does not care about class and gender differences, she was able to make friends with all the men of the village. She is described as a frequenter of male specific cafes and taverns, where she even buys drinks for her male friends.

> *"Nevin spoke to everyone in the village [Beykoz]. People seeing her entering traditional cafes (kahve), or even taverns (meyhane), would not see the need to gossip. Only a few would grumble. Everyone knew that Consul Vildan Bey's daughter was educated abroad and was a tomboy."*

It is apparent that she had some sort of a protective shield in her native village/town, because of common knowledge of her background and who she is. However, she was also daring enough to have two glasses of cognac in a male beer-house in Ankara, without minding her womanhood ("kadınlığına bakmadan"). Apart from her insistence in entering these homosocial male spaces, as a defiance of the gender rules imposed upon women, Nevin is also described as the direct opposite of a proper lady in her everyday behavior in public places. While a good-looking and respectable couple watches the Bosphorus on the sea shore, she would sit on the bollard on the pier and comb her hair with her fingers, or else would pick her teeth with a matchstick. While the stylish ladies waited for the ferry, she would take a bite from a quince and ask the dockman to hit her on the back, when it

Encounters and Body Work in Turkish Beauty Salons," *Journal of the Middle East Women's Studies* 12/2 (2016): 181-202.

stick in her throat.[40] These lines describe the extraordinariness of Nevin especially when compared to elegant and dignified women. Nevin refuses to act on the dictates of femininity, determined by the social class to which she belongs. Here it is important to note that gender performances are not determined in vacuum, rather they are shaped by other factors such as social class, ethnicity, age, and others. In that respect, the resistance or difference of characters such as Eleni, Katina, or Melek, as members of subordinate classes was of a different order than Nevin.

Nevin is also declaredly in conflict with the forms of behavior that are deemed appropriate for women in male-female relationships. When a young man makes her a compliment, she refuses to act accordingly, saying she "does not like to assume a lady attitude" (57). In another instance, she warns her boyfriend Cemal not to act like a womanizer. She wants him to speak to her in a manly manner (*erkekçe*), as if they are two male friends (9). With this intervention, she makes it clear that she is determined to challenge the expected gender performances in a heterosexual relationship. There are no detailed descriptions of the facial and bodily features of Nevin in the novel. There are a few times where the narrator mentions her bright, white teeth and her big, long-fingered hands. In the last lines of the novel, the character's appearance is described as if in an expressionist painting. However, this quick mirror image of the woman leaves no doubt that the attire of Nevin was quite masculine.

> *"She got up, put a beret in her head, tossed on her male trench-coat that she always wore. As she was walking out of the door, she saw something mud-colored, blue, purple thing in the mirror of the coat hanger. Within this gray, blue, and purple, her face without make-up was the pale face of a school boy." (80)*

Nevin, as a female protagonist contradicts all gender stereotypes dictated by the society. However, Sait Faik creates a character that demands not only equality for women, but also room for differences, even queerness. In that respect, Nevin represents not only women, but also other marginalized people, who assume or aspire for "another thought, another nature (*tabiat*), another morality, another disposition (*yaradılış*)" (17), and who therefore are drawn away from the majority.

## CONCLUSION

Queer theory views the traditional and essentialist model of sexuality as inadequate in understanding how desires function and how sexualities are made. It argues that thinking in terms of a single and coherent sexuality (either heterosexual or homosexual) is an essentialist conception that still

---

40 "...iskelenin üstünde belediye doktorunun genç, şık karısıyla konuşurken babanın üstüne oturur, saçını parmağı ile tarar, dişini kibrit çöpü ile karıştırır, şık hanımların vapur beklediği salonda sonbaharda, inci gibi dişleriyle ayva ısırırken boğazında kalırsa çımacıya sırtını yumruklatır..."

condemns other sexualities as "perverse". Queer theory, in that sense, is also philosophical challenge to the status quo, aiming to undermine sameness and praise otherness.

Sait Faik is incredibly exceptional in his capability to create and embrace a range of queer characters. As much as it is a futile effort to search for elaborate gay desires, or anachronistically open gay characters in his works, he offers the reader a range of queer characters, ready to bend essentialist modes of gender and sexuality in their everyday performances. Eve Kosofsky Sedgwick recalled in the 1990s that in a class she was teaching at Amherst College, half of her students said they have read and studied Oscar Wilde's Dorian Gray in previous classes, but there was never any discussion of the book's homosexual content. It is no surprise that Sait Faik's works, almost after eighty years of readership and considerable fame, have only marginally been read through the glances of gender and sexuality. Literary criticism focused on several other aspects of his works and issues such as sexuality, queerness, and gender performativity remained largely "in the closet".

## REFERENCES

Andrews, W. G. & M. Kalpaklı (2005) The Age of Beloveds: Love and the Beloved in Early-Modern Ottoman and European Culture and Society. Durham: Duke University Press.

Arık, H. (2009) "Kahvehanede Erkek Olmak: Kamusal Alanda Erkek Egemenliğin Antropolojisi," 168-201. In *Cins Cins Mekân*. Edited by Ayten Alkan. Istanbul: Varlık.

Belge, M. (1998) "Eşcinsellik." In *Edebiyat Üstüne Yazılar*, 446-52. Istanbul: İletişim.

Butler, J. (1992) Gender Trouble: Feminism and the Subversion of Identity. New York: Routledge.

Butler, J. (1997) *The Psychic Life of Power: Theories in Subjection*. California: Stanford University Press.

Çakırlar, C. & S. Delice (2012) eds. Cinsellik Muamması: Türkiye'de Queer Kültür ve Muhalefet. Istanbul: Metis.

Cebeci, O. (2004) *Psikanalitik Edebiyat Kuramı*. Istanbul: İthaki.

Halperin, D. M. (1990) One Hundred Years of Homosexuality and Other Essays on Greek Love. London: Routledge.

Dynes, W. R. & S. Donaldson (1992) eds. *Homosexual Themes in Literary Studies*. New York: Garland.

Güven, O. (2010) "Sait Faik'in Hikaye ve Romanlarında Homoerotizm, Erkek İmgesi Kadın Temsilleri." Unpublished MA Thesis, Bilkent University.

Halman, T. S. (1995) "Introduction: Fiction of a Flâneur," 3-11. In *A Dot On The Map: Selected Stories And Poems*. Bloomington: Indiana University Turkish Studies.

Halman, T. S. (2004) "Preface." In *Sleeping in the Forest: Stories and Poems*, vii-viii. Syracuse: Syracuse University Press.

Kellogg, S. (1983) ed. *Literary Visions of Homosexuality*. New York: Haworth.

Landry, D. (2014) "Queering Identities in Ottoman History and Turkish Identity," 215-243. In *Turkey and the Politics of National Identity: Social, Economic and Cultural Transformation*. Edited by Shane Brennan, Marc Herzog. New York: I.B. Tauris.

Liebelt, C. (2016) "Grooming Istanbul: Intimate Encounters and Body Work in Turkish Beauty Salons." *Journal of the Middle East Women's Studies* 12(2): 181-202.

Malinowski, S. & C. Brelin (1995) The Gay and Lesbian Literary Heritage: A Reader's

Companion to the Writers and Their Works, from Antiquity to the Present. New York: Holt.

Meyer, M. (1994) ed. *The Politics and Poetics of Camp*. New York: Routledge.

Meyers, J. (1977) *Homosexuality and Literature, 1890-1930*. London: Athlone Press.

Naci, F. (2003) *Sait Faik'in Hikâyeciliği*. İstanbul: Yapı Kredi.

Oğuzertem, S. (2004) "Introduction: Sait Faik's Utopian Poetics and the Lyrical Turn in Turkish Fiction." In *Sleeping in the Forest: Stories and Poems*, xv-xxx. Syracuse: Syracuse University Press.

Oktay, A. (1992) "Kabul ve Red: Yalnızlığın Kutupları," 83-98. In *Kabul ve Red*. İstanbul: Simavi.

Osborne, P. & L. Segal (1994) "Gender as Performance: An Interview with Judith Butler." conducted by Peter Osborne and Lynne Segal, *Radical Philosophy* 67: 32-39.

Pollard, P. (1991) *Andre Gide: Homosexual Moralist*. London: Yale University Press.

Sedgwick Kosofsky, E. (1985) *Between Men: English Literature and Male Homosocial Desire*. New York: Columbia University Press.

Sedgwick Kosofsky, E. (1990) *Epistemology of the Closet*. Berkeley: University of California Press.

Selden, R., P. Widdowson & P. Brooker (2005) *A Reader's Guide to Contemporary Literary Theory*. Harlow: Pearson Longman.

Stokes, M. (2010) The Republic of Love: Cultural Intimacy in Turkish Popular Music. Chicago: University of Chicago Press.

Türker, Y. (2008) "Bir Serüven." *Kaos GL*, 102: 14.

Woods, G. (1998) *A History of Gay Literature: The Male Tradition*. New Haven: Yale University Press.

# CHAPTER 7

# AN ANALYSIS OF THE CINEMATIC REPRESENTATION OF LGBT: LOLA AND BILLY THE KID

Ayçin Alp and Çağlar Özbek

In societies, the concept of "biological sex" has been used to describe male and female genders. In this case, which points to a dual system, LGBT (lesbian-gay-bisexual-transgender) individuals are considered as disadvantaged groups and are pushed out of norm, based on heteronormative norms. In the heteronormative society model, LGBT individuals are characterized by many prejudicial expressions such as "perverted", "pervert", "diseased". In this structure, LGBT individuals, labeled as "the other", can face life and rights violations, along with their isolation from the public space.

In order to create awareness, increase visibility of LGBT individuals in the society and solve their problems; along with LGBT organizations, the non-profit organizations, independent initiatives, the artists have also made great efforts. In particular, the functions of the cinema, such as showing the social realities that are not seen or ignored, and raising consciousness / awareness on the social ground has caused cinema to reach the society rapidly as a result of its being both visual and auditory.

It is possible to mention the movies that are about the lives of LGBT individuals both in Turkey and worldwide. As addressing the problems of Turkish families that migrated to Germany, Turkish German co-produced movie "Lola and Billy the Kid" directed by Kutluğ Ataman is also important in terms of showing the representation of being LGBT in diaspora. Centering the concepts like migration, identity, homophobia and otherness, this study aims a descriptive analysis of LGBT individuals' representations in cinema through Kutluğ Ataman's film "Lola and Billy The Kid".

## INTRODUCTION

Engagement of cinema in sociology has become an issue, frequently argued on both universally and nationally, in Turkey, especially in the post-1980 era, where the world had evolved. Cinematic representation of social realities has been the research subject of various disciplines as well. Communication specialists, sociologists and even politicians vastly concentrate on the engagement of cinema, as a visually authored textbook, in social realities. The cinema, pointing at a mechanism of semiosis assisted by semiotics offers a chance to analyse the society.

In this respect, this study, also being grounded on the cinematic and sociological contexts, aims to analyse the cinematic representation of LGBT individuals, with a historical perspective, addresses the cinematic representation of LGBT in Turkey, and conducts a text analysis on "Lola and Billy The Kid", a movie by Kutluğ Ataman, a Turkish director. Both in media and in cinema, as an artistic style of expression, the real-life reflections of LGBT individuals, tend to gather around victimisation and problems encountered, in general. However, art should enable the alienated to express their existence as well as all the other realities. Because, despite its varying objectives, which, in deed, does not harm it, art reflects the reality. Through art, human-beings recognise the world and seizes the power to change it (Yamaner, 2009:141). Therefore, artistic activities and pieces, introduced without deviating from the primary objective of art, have the power to raise awareness.

Problems such as the social status of LGBT individuals, the oppression they are exposed to and the violence against them, the pressure by both the society and the state due to their sexual orientation and identity, the difficulties they run into in their careers, the rough nature of survival as an immigrant in another country are implicitly introduced to the audience through cinema. This conveying nature of cinema provides a means to tell the society about the claims of LGBT individuals on "their sexual rights, earning their lives, gaining their sexual freedom and being a part of the society" (Selek, 2011:185). Not limited to this, the primary function of cinema, as well as reflecting the reality of such victimisations and raising a public awareness for prevention thereof, should be to help LGBT individuals survive naturally as everyone else does.

Not only the cinematic representation of such realities regarding LGBT, in particular, is fundamental in terms of guiding the society, but also the analysis of films produced both in Turkish, and in European and American cinema, being committed, directly or indirectly, to homosexuality, with a historical perspective, would make it possible to make predictions on where the LGBT individuals are situated in cinema.

## CINEMATOGRAPHY: A MODERN NARRATIVE

Having started in the early 1800s, with the incorporation of text and motion, cinematography has become a form of art pertaining to motion pictures. Cinematography, resembling the working principles of an aircraft, has a nature that makes motion and transition between scenes possible. That is, although once flying was a dream, it has become insignificant, and cinema, gradually, has had the power to manufacture dreams. (Diken and Laustsen, 2011:19). Cinema, being also referred to as a "dream factory", is a part of visual arts, addressing the human vision just as the poems and music address the human audition, serves the art's purpose of rehabilitating the senses for a better understanding of the world (Farago, 2011:21). This, on the other hand, does not mean a film is an artistic activity that is there just to entertain us or distract our attention.

*Cinema functions as a social unconsciousness in a way: interprets, reproduces, displaces bends the object of social analysis. Cinema does not only introduce ideas on societies, it is also an integral part of those societies it pictures. However, cinema does not only reflect/bend an external reality, but also provides the social life with a vast universe of probabilities. In this respect, cinema is mostly an experiment conducted in evolving society. (Diken and Laustsen, 2011:24)*

The invention by Lumière brothers in 1895, where they discovered the harmony of a lightweight recorder and the projector, has possessed one of the most important assets in the world; the re-presentation of motion. And this made it possible to build a historical bridge between cinema and the reality (Barnouw cited in Carmona, 2016:202). That is, with cinema's contribution to social history, and the Industrial Revolution, beside the traditional narratives, the works of recent narratives began to project the representations of social life (Abisel, 1999:17). However, in the modern society, it is a must to consider films as not only the projectors but also the builders of meanings (Koç, 2008:4).

Most of the time, foundations of films are laid on a soil of fiction; it is possible to consider this in the manner what is depicted by Aragon as "*true lying*", though. And as such mentioned by Žižek, even when films lie, they tell the lie which dwells in the very heart of our social edifice (cited in Diken and Laustsen, 2011:15). Observed from this perspective, the art of cinema relates to picture no more, but forms a new world to project the truth (Farago, 2011:27). This newly formed world is such that it projects the reality in a dark room, allegorically with fiction and fantasies in a way. That fiction and the fantasies travels through the reality. Žižek argues that fantasies are not illusions for escaping from reality; he rather describes them as the actual foundations of social life. Therefore, according to Žižek, the greatest achievement cinema is not that it recreates reality in a fictional narrative, allures and makes us perceive the fiction as the reality, but that it makes us experience the reality as fiction. As a result, the relation between the social theory and films are as dim as those between fiction and non-fiction, or representation and reality. Diken and Laustsen, in an effort to leap beyond questioning the films over the incompatibility of social reality with fiction or vice versa, employ a cinematical social theory with their concept of socio-fiction. This makes it possible to analyse the films allegorically as social events, rather than the depiction and analysis of social facts through abstract theories (2011:34). This method of analysis allows the interpretation of latent patterns and ideologies under the fiction title.

The social events in films are mostly based on an ideology and are shaped by the ideas of directors. However, beginning from the 1990s, Hollywood, trying to make a film popular over its director only, lead to a criticism that one director alone may not create a film. Therefore, the idea of directors taking full control of their films is practically founded on a loose soil, and social, political and economical perspectives of both them and their crew have been considered among the factors that influence the films (Kabadayı, 2013:113).

Cinema, endowing a unique soil for manufacturing ideologies, may, from time to time, manufactures the truth through the representations consolidated by supporting the sovereign ideology, whereas it may create alternative representations for the rest of the time. Cinematic sociology, being attached to the manner, which the events arising out of social realities are represented, as well, is aware of the fact that most of the time, the manners of representation are shaped by the ideologies of cinema that possess the sovereignty within society. Thus, there are problems emerging with respect to how much of the truth a film tells and how much of the reality it represents. There is a probability, where, from time to time, the audience dogmatically accept the relation between representation and reality, without a critical approach, and stay focused on a film passively depending on the ideology of the director only. And this may result in negative outcomes such as the formation of prejudice in the society or firm judgements. Especially the screenwriters, who have an important role with respect to this reality and representation, become unaware of the fact that they create an unreal perception in the society and convey messages that do not represent reality, due to the concerns of having humour elements in their character choice, or commercial concerns. Therefore, defining the identities to be represented (e.g. sexual, ethnicity, nationality etc.) beforehand is important and that the concepts are handled through a literature review rather than superficially, and the scenarios are written with respect thereto, would provide an opportunity to produce realistic films that could mirror the society.

## LGBT REPRESENTATION IN EUROPEAN AND AMERICAN CINEMA

Contrary to Turkish cinema, the first representations of homosexuality in American cinema, began with the release of productions on male homosexuality (Öğüt and Deniz, 2012:68). Starting from the birth of cinema, Hollywood has always placed an importance on homosexuality, however, during different periods, the meaning of homosexuality and how it is represented in the cinema have varied. Especially during the 1930s and 1940s, homosexuality had been projected as a miserable, ridiculous and even a frightening behaviour, and the films produced included homophobic discourse, whether latently or directly.

40 years after Stonewall Riots and 30 years after the emergence of HIV-AIDS as a social and a public health problem, independent and main stream films included queer scenes more. This experiment, narrative styles, themes and New Queer Cinema (NQC) in an intense phase of LGBTI activism, provided a set of visual representations and ideological edifices that could provide a basis for discussions on queer theory in a climate of phobic culture with ideological concerns, in academical, political, artistic and cultural contexts (Jones and Juett, 2010:ix). NQC, in particular, has the characteristic of being an extension of an activist movement that desires to challenge a homophobic cultural history.

Looking back in the history of cinema, one of the primitive experiments of the early queer cinema was "The Gay Brothers", an American film by Thomas Edison in 1895. Two men dancing and a third man playing a violin, despite not being a complete LGBTI representation, had the characteristic of being one of the first steps in this respect. And in fact, homosexuality was a humour element in the film. In the late 1920s and early 1930s on the other hand, lesbianism was included, and the first movie with lesbianism theme, "Pandora's Box", was produced in 1929. However, in the mid 1930s, in parallel with the Hays Code, Hollywood decided to censor its own productions. This, on the other hand, had not cause representation of homosexuality to vanish completely but caused the directors to conceal their implications of homosexuality. Having become worse in 1950s with the "masculine" policy, the rage against gays increased drastically (Davies, 2010:23-27). In 1960s, homosexuals were depicted as "horrible individuals", "reprobates", "individuals with evil backgrounds", "miserable" or at the very least "suicidal".

In 32 films produced in the USA and the UK between 1961-1967, 13 homosexual characters commit suicides and 18 were killed by other characters (Ulusay, 2011:3). Despite the manner, that was the first time where so many homosexual individuals were represented in the cinema of 1960s, however, while such individuals liberalized, those in the cinema could not be liberalized. Hollywood, due to the restrictions of 1960s, projected a negative representation (Benshoff and Griffin, 2004:8).

*In September 1961, Motion Picture Association of America announced that they amended the Production Code: The Code allowed onscreen homosexuality, as long as it was treated with 'care, discretion, and restraint' (Davies, 2010:68-69).*

In the mid 1960s on the other hand, many actors, screenwriters and producers tended to produce underground films in West Side of New York. This way, three avant-garde films, "Scorpio Rising" by Kenneth Anger, "Flaming Creatures" by Jack Smith and "Christmas on Earth" by Barbara Rubin, each having an important place in queer cinema, were produced in 1963. During this period, where a sexual revolution had also occurred, Andy Warhol produced many works, as well (Davies, 2010:70-71). Andy Warhol, who has been considered as one of the pioneers of pop-art movement, has been recognised with his radical representations of homosexual identities in his short films.

It is possible to say that homosexual individuals, who could not be liberated until those years, became more apparent in the public subsequent to Stonewall Riots in 1969. Thereafter, although it was not explicit, with the media's support there had been some changes in the attitudes towards them. With world's transition to a politically more liberal ideology, there were more characters included, symbolising homosexuality "positively" and an awareness was raised in cinema. "The Boys in the Band" by Mart Cowley, which was released in the same period with activist homosexual movement, tries to tell Americans about the challenges experienced by male homosexuals (Davies, 2010:94-97). Especially with the campaigns by the activists in the USA, the American Psychiatric Association's ruling on homosexuality in 1974, which stated that homosexuality is not a disease, has become a milestone (Benshoff and Griffin, 2004:4). In a stage where cinematic representation of homosexuality was no longer a problem, outbreak of AIDS led to another strong resistance against homosexuality in the 1980s. The tabloid media in England depicted homosexuals as virus carriers and Thatcher Government, instead of raising awareness and revealing the truths about the disease, proposed the Article 28 on preventing Municipalities from supporting materials concerning homosexuality. Although that was the situation, the best film in 1980s with an LGBT theme was produced not in Hollywood but in Europe. Especially in the film "My Beautiful Laundrette", gay males in English cinema, stepped into a historical period where they challenged the system, social justice and middle-class morality. In the USA in mid 1980s an "AIDS Cinema" emerged in the same period with independent films, and this cinema included scenes exploiting emotions, and homosexuals were introduced as "victims" (Davies, 2010:138-142). As parts of AIDS activism, both media and LGBT cultures started changing with motives such as technological advancement, globalisation and profit making (Rich, 2013:89). In this respect, Hok and Leung argued that this Independent Cinema in the USA was commoditised by Hollywood with global heterosexist capitalist approach (2004:157). In 1990s, as a response to AIDS generation in a way, transphobia rose, and LGBT individuals were commoditised as elements of comedy.

The films produced in 90s constituted the "new queer cinema" and especially the films such as The Hours and Times (Christopher Munch,

1991), Swoon (Tom Kalin, 1991), The Living End (Gregg Araki, 1992) ve R.S.V.P (Laurie Lynd, 1992) have been the milestones for gay and lesbian cinema, in San Francisco Gay and Lesbian Film Festival (Rich, 1995:164). In the 2000s on the other hand, homosexual cinema made itself more apparent and achieved great successes. With queer cinema year, led by Hollywood, March 5th, 2006 went down in history as "Homosexual Oscars". In Golden Globe Awards, 4 awards wnet to the film "Brokeback Mountain" and 6 awards went to gay and transsexual characters (Davies, 2010:254-255).

## TURKISH CINEMA AND THE OTHERS

The heterosexist structure, which is shaped by social norms, established its dominance on visual texts such as cinema. Therefore, despite the fact that the history of cinema dates back to the 1800s, the examination of the nature and subject of the films shows that LGBT individuals are introduced covertly, and they were able appear in Turkish cinema only after 1960s. However, "Ver Elini İstanbul", the first film to introduce homosexuality in Turkey, not significantly though, was released in 1962. The film, which was directed by Aydın Arakon and written by Atilla İlhan with the false name Ali Kaptanoğlu, introduced two women kissing innocently in a scene, for the first time. In addition, films such as "İki Gemi Yanyana", "Harem'de Dört Kadın" included female homosexuality in 1960s (Avcı, 2013). However, they were not based directly on homosexuality, but introduced innocent intimacies. As the stories in those films were not composed of "different" sexual identities, they may not be considered as the pioneers in terms of how homosexuality was introduced.

Between the years 1974-79, with the sex rush in films, women's sexuality and homosexuality in cinema was used as a means of sexual exploitation. Especially in these films, which were screened for male audience, sometimes women kissing were shown with commercial motives. In general, in the films produced after the 80s, the lesbian identity was fully addressed; instead, lesbianism was introduced in a male-oriented manner, suggesting that women were victimized by men develop intimacy with their same-sex partners. In "Düş Gezginleri", a film by Atıf Yılmaz in 1992 (the first Turkish film to participate in the International Torino Gay and Lesbian Film Festival), once again, lesbianism was introduced as an intimacy established between women who were victimized by men (Öğüt ve Deniz: 2012:68-70).

In 80s, the military coup had its impressions on cinema as well and imposed some sanctions. The film "Beddua" in 1980, where Bülent Ersoy acted in before changing sex, was the first film with male homosexuality theme. However, the film introduced an individual, who was raped in his childhood, and changed sex as he could not endure the situation, and therefore associated homosexuality with the rape incident rather than emotions, feelings or orientation. In the film "Yüz Karası", directed by

Orhan Aksoy in 1981, where Bülent Ersoy acted again, the reasons of homosexuality were introduced as being raped in childhood, playing with baby dolls, just as in the film "Beddua", with the dominance of coup. In this film homosexuality was introduced as heresy/perversion, and at the end of the film Bülent Ersoy, changing sex again to be a male, appealed for mercy in a way. "Acılar Paylaşılmaz" by Eser Zorlu, has similarities with Ersoy's films, as it introduces a father who tries to discourage his homosexual son and associates homosexuality with paternal issues.

Another group in the history of Turkish cinema is transsexuals and transvestites. Francesca Bertini, the first actress in the history of cinema to play a man, featured in an Italian film, Histoire D'Pierrot. In Turkey on the other hand, transvestites were introduced for the first time in a 1923 film "Leblebici Horhor" directed by Muhsin Ertuğrul. But here as well, the representation of homosexuality could not be matter of discussion, and the scenarios written on transvestites are also problematic in representation (Özgüç, 2000: 53). In fact, transvestites appeared as elements of comedy, and these films are about women or men who disguise to overcome some difficult situations. Especially male characters change into a female character for a short time and in the end, they change into male characters again. In the Turkish films, transvestism was mostly continued with manly female characters after 1959. This trend, having become a fashion, started with "Fosforlu Cevriye", featured by Neriman Köksal. After that, Sezer Sezin in "Şoför Nebahat", Leyla Sayar in "Aslan Yavrusu", Belgin Doruk in "Gece Kuşu" and Fatma Girik in "Belalı Torun" became the masculine characters. Again, just as lesbianism was the first to be introduced in cinema in terms of homosexual relationships, the roles of transvestites were featured by women initially, and it was 40 years that when men appeared in cinema. In the film "Fıstık Gibi Maşallah", directed by Hulki Soner in 1964, and featured by Sadri Alışık and İzzet Günay, the primary elements were transvestites, however, they still played men who were in trouble and disguised, and eventually changed back to their male identities (Özgüç, 2000:54). Thus, being a transvestite has been considered a temporary incident and the "alienation" of transvestites had become a common perception of audience. In conclusion, the main objective of these films in featuring transvestite identities, was to "amuse" the audience.

Around 1993, homosexuality, which was introduced superficially and not as a main theme previously, has been addressed for the first time. Although "Gece, Melek ve Bizim Çocuklar", a film by Atıf Yılmaz, treats homosexuality as a side theme and the homosexuals as "out-of-the-norms" personalities, it treats them more courageously, when compared to previous productions. The trend of introducing both homosexuals and transvestites as an amusement element, which lasted until 1993, was left aside and treated as reality of life. Especially with the impression of independent cinema emerging in 90s, the perspectives of cinema professionals regarding the issue has changed, and thereafter homosexuality has been told through "friendship". For instance, in the film "Hamam", directed by Ferzan Özpetek in 1997, the gay identity was addressed through friendship. Similary in Özpetek's other films such as "Cahil Periler", "Serseri Mayınlar" and "Bir Ömür Yetmez", homosexuality was addressed with a prominent "friendship" theme. 5 films by Turkish directors, were chosen by Kaos GL Magazine among the 100 films with LGBT theme. These films are Düş Gezginleri (Atıf Yılmaz, 1992), İki Genç Kız (Kutluğ Ataman, 2004), Lola and Billy The Kid (Kutluğ Ataman, 1999), Cahil Periler (Ferzan Özpetek, 2001) and Gece, Melek ve Bizim Çocuklar (Atıf Yılmaz, 1993) (Safoğlu, 2008a:74-77). What needs to be addressed here is that Kutluğ Ataman and Ferzan Özpetek are directors living outside Turkey. Thus, the facts that they obtained most of their capital for the films outside Turkey, often use countries other than Turkey as film venue, the films were first released in other countries other than Turkey, are important in terms of re-establishing the reality reflected by these films.

In addition to these films, Zenne is one of the most important films with LGBT theme in modern Turkish Cinema. This film is about homosexuality of Ahmet Yıldız, and murder of his father due to him not abiding by social norms, was shot in 2008 by Ahmet Caner Alper and Mehmet Binay, friends of Yıldız, and released in 2011. In addition to addressing this hate crime in the film, the Turkish Armed Forces' perspective on homosexuality is reflected in all its reality.

Another important example is the feature-length documentary titled "Benim Çocuğum", directed by Can Candan in 2013, in which parents of LGBT individuals tell their life stories at first-hand. With this film, parents who have been organized under LISTAG (LGBTT Families Istanbul Group) tried to reach a wide audience in order to raise awareness in society by expressing the troubles they experienced.

Although there were exceptions before the 2000s, it can be seen that LGBT representation had not been introduced to the society in the Turkish cinema with its realities, but rather with commercial concerns, as an element of humour exploiting sexuality, or with the concept of "friendship". Cinema, which reflects the reality of the society and act a mirror of each period in a way, had not achieved its full purpose in the case of LGBT individuals. It had not only been unable to fulfil its objectives, but also might have led homophobia and transphobia in the society to become stronger, as it deviated from its objectives, treated homosexuals as elements of humour and introduced them as perverts / heretics and freaks.

## THE BACKGROUND OF "LOLA AND BILLY THE KID"

The 1880s are accepted as the years when the cinema industry began to emerge. From these years until the present day, there are not many examples of homosexual cinema. Some examples in the hand present the identity or orientation as a representation outside of reality. Sometimes the LGBT was introduced as diseased, perverted/deviant, directly or implicitly due to any reactions from the society. However, in most cases, they became the elements of humour in cinema, and were humiliated through their sexuality. While this was the case, the films that show the truth in all its transparency, such as Lola and Billy the Kid, have an important place in the history of homosexual cinema.

Lola and Billy The Kid were shot in Berlin by Kutluğ Ataman who was born in Istanbul. In the film, Ataman casted unrecognized names instead of creating a popular cast. Except for Hasan Ali Mete featuring Osman, Erdal Yıldız featuring Billy the Kid and Baki Davrak featuring Murat, all actors were chosen among the Turks, who were not professionals and lived in Germany. Although Ataman wanted to shoot the film in Turkey, the film was shot in Germany with some funding, due to failure to find a sponsor in Turkey. Moreover, it is no coincidence that Ataman shot the film in Berlin. The speech of Karl Heinrich Ulrichs defending homosexual rights at the German Lawyers Congress in Munich in August 1867 was accepted as the beginning of the homosexual liberation movement in Germany. Again, in Berlin, the sexologist Marcus Hirschfeld founded the Institute of Sexual Sciences, but the 12 thousand books, 35 thousand photographs and countless manuscripts in his library were destroyed by the Nazi students on 6 May 1933 (Baird, 2004: 27-28). Germany and Berlin in particular are considered as one of the most important centres in which homosexual movement was born and developed. Therefore, it can be said that the country and city that the director has chosen for the film has turned out to be a conscious choice.

The film, which opened Panorama Section of the Berlin Film Festival, as Ataman describes, was "an early film" for Turkey of 1998. Because the film approaches prejudice on sexual and racial identities in the context of "German Turks", and due to the inclusion of sexuality theme, it became one of the films that could lead to "misunderstanding" in daytime cinema of the public. However, the film won awards in Turin, Oslo and Istanbul (which Ataman reports in his interview with Mithat Alam that it was possible with the contributions of homosexuals, Alam, 2009:14), and The Best Film Award in the New Festival in New York.

Ataman, pointing to a platform in which reality and fiction collide in his films, enables the subject to construct, realize and resolve itself (Pullen, 2012: 360). In this respect, being free of commercial concerns unlike the popular cinema, he opened a realistic window to the narratives of the society which are being neglected. Instead of addressing a single social event or phenomenon, the film reflects the many realities of society to the audience, and embraced numerous concepts such as the migration of Turks to Germany and the survival of the Turks living in Germany, the individuals who are isolated from the society due to their ethnical and sexual identities and/or orientations, the hate speech and crime, and the social classes. The film is important both as a Turkish director, for the first time, introduces sexual identities by including authentic representations and the film is a period drama shot in Berlin, a spot where the sexual revolution emerged painfully.

## AN IMMIGRATION STORY: "THE GERMAN TURKS"

Towards the end of the 1950s, Germany let approximately two million workers in as immigrants, from Turkey, where the majority of those are from, Greece, Portugal, Spain and Yugoslavia. When combined, the labour shortage in German industry developing in post-WWII period and the unseen and prominent unemployment in Turkey, evolved into a massive labour flow from Turkey, a movement of migration towards the Federal Republic of Germany, in early 1960s (Turan, 1997 13). This migration occurred due to economic difficulties or miscellaneous reasons. Due to their cultural differences and lifestyles, immigrants encountered some difficulties as they were unable integrate into a new society and the culture that belongs to it. What is meant by integration is that the ethnic, social and minority groups in a social edifice should have equal access to all opportunities in that country and should be able to live without any conflicts. As a matter of fact, the reason why this integration process has failed, results from the facts that individuals, although not arbitrarily, continue their relations with their country of origin, and therefore do not lose their national identity (Tuna and Özbek, 2012: 47). Thus, the integration of the Turks into the German society became more difficult due to their preserved identity, and the Turks were subjected to an intense marginalization by the majority of Germans. This situation led to the formation of Turkish neighbourhoods, as the Turks living in Germany tended to live together closely, with a sense of unity. The principle of being neighbours is an important structural sign in these neighbourhoods, which has evolved into communities by taking an origin-based form of settlement and organization. Thus, being neighbours is primarily related to a relationship resulting from living in immediate vicinities and based on the values arising therefrom rather than relationship by affinity (Gezgin, 2013: 185).

Although Turks live in their local space and in conformance to their national identity, and style their lives accordingly, it has not been possible to prevent dominance of Germans on and their assimilation policies regarding Turks, as the Germans dominate public areas, treat the Turks differently due to their religion, language and race, and as second-class citizens by hiring them as unskilled labours.

Especially the banning of Turkish language in 2010 in various locations of Germany, the Turkish language course being a mandatory or credit course no more, or even removed, has become an attempt of assimilation the Turks strongly reacted against. However, Esser states that in order for an integration into system for the purpose of a more homogenous society, it is not a must that these new members of the society know the language or become assimilated into the cultures or groups they live in as long as the immigrants pay their taxes and abide by the laws (2000: 56-66). Nevertheless, although not a requirement, in the current system people are supposed to harmonise with the German society due to the needs such as survival, providing education for their children etc.

## IS THAT YOUR REAL HAIR?

Stuart Hall studied the correlation between representation, language and culture, placing an importance on the concepts of representation and the others. Hall, stating "Representation is about telling something meaningful by using the language or present the world to other people in a meaningful manner" further expresses that representation is an integral part of the process where the meaning is manufactured and shared among the members of a culture, and that it includes the use of language, representation or replacement of things by or with signs or images (Hall cited in Kırel, 2010:364-65). In this respect, the wig, which Ataman places an emphasis in his film and in his book *Peruk Takan Kadınlar* (2001) as well, has the nature of representation that manufactures a meaning. The wig, which appears in the film with Lola's making an appearance for the first time, appears multiple times during the film.

Considering the purposes of using a wig, it might be an accessory that individuals wear to hide their identity, could hide behind like curtain from time to time, as a requirement or due to their religious beliefs. Moreover, a wig (one that is made of real human hair), when considered as an accessory that Lola uses to hide the transvestite identity, may mean to carry someone else's DNA and to assume someone else's identity, instead of one's own. Accordingly, Lola is at defence by associating himself with the place where he feels that he belongs in the public and creating the identity of his choice, through his attitudes, speech, style, dressing and wig, in particular, to change and rebuild his identity that is attacked by the oppressive and authoritarian society (Baykal, 2008:44). In this respect, wig represents Lola's sexual identity and his revolt against heteronormativity. Lola makes an appearance especially with his red wig, when he wants to reveal his sexual identity to his family, and tell his brother's shame, who raped him to suppress his homosexuality, in his face. Furthermore, in another scene, one of the German teens, who are homophobic and constantly attacks Lola with hate speeches, and saying "Bring me that Turk's wig..!" reveals that wig does not only represent but also symbolises.

Where the male-dominated system is appreciated so much, it is "embarrassing" and "humiliating" for an individual lacking dominant masculine codes, to give up the "supreme" masculinity and become effeminate. Therefore, in the reactions against lesbians or bisexuals, not much hate speech is involved when compared to those against gay and transsexual individuals, as lesbians do not have a male identity that they could give up, or a bisexual, although not completely, is still considered a male. From a heterosexist perspective, human with a universally assigned sex desires the opposite sex in general, and also is dependent on that desired one to fertilise. The desire for the same sex is just coincidental and is an exception that does not break the rules. Therefore, in traditional societies, marriages and the tendency to have children proves an individual a male or female. In other words, the concepts of male and female is not only predefined but also determined by the formation of a family (Agacinski, 1998:79-81). In the film as well, even though Bili is a gay, acting like a stereotype Turkish macho man and asking Lola to change his sex to a female, makes an emphasis on the concept of traditional family, and wants to marry and make a "housewife" out of "the prospective her" in Turkey. Because he is humiliated by Lola's sexual identity when he runs into an acquaintance in the public, and as he is the active party in his speeches, he makes an emphasis on that he could not be called a "fairy". In this way, it is possible to consider Bili as a homosexual, who wants to hide this identity, and who is also a latent homophobic, whereas Osman, Lola's brother, as a latent homosexual and an extremely homophobic character, who dares to kill his brother.

Similar to Bili, İskender also denies his homosexuality in his relationship with Friedrich and expresses homophobia by calling Friedrich a "fairy". Ataman addresses the concepts of social class and status through the relationship between İskender and Friedrich. Especially in Friedrich's conversation with his mother, Ute, on his relationship, the mother, instead of giving judgements on his son's sexual orientation, criticises İskender's social status. What Ataman places an emphasis on here is that a come-out situation, an act of revealing identity, which would certainly end up with being thrown out of the house and disinherited, and even fratricide in a Turkish family, could be discussed comfortably in a European family.

## YOUR SEX? MALE (M) OR FEMALE (F)

In the early 1900s, Berlin was a city to have offered the utmost rights and liberties for homosexuals. However, with the Article 175, where a provision on banning sexual intercourse between males involved, appended to German Criminal Code, this had changed, and sexual liberties were restricted. Especially with Adolf Hitler having come into the power, many scientific researches on sexual identities were ceased, homosexual bars and night clubs were shut down, and the Nazis conducted a terror campaign against the homosexuals (Wolf, 2012:55). In 1933, in Holocaust, which is also known as

Jewish Massacre, particularly homosexuals in Nazi Government were killed, and between 1933-45 around 100.000 homosexuals were arrested and 50.000 of those were officially convicted. Many of those were marked with pink triangles (which later became the symbol of gay liberation), castrated according to the provisions of European court upon being sent to concentration camps, and tortured. With the abolishment of Article 175 in 1994, registered partnership has been made official in 2001[1]. That Ataman themed homosexuality in Germany, which has such a dark history, and especially in Berlin, is associated with their history. As the plot takes place in Berlin in 1999, it refers to a transition period. However, this transition period has not managed to eliminate homophobia, and the film touches on this issue in particular. Lola, despite striving for building his identity in a more favourable habitat when compared to Turkey, he was said to be killed by Germans due to his ethnicity, however found out to be killed by his homophobic brother. Apart from Osman, a homophobic homosexual, the film introduces a teen from the German teen group, one of the harassers of Lola. This teen, even though he seems to try to trap Murat, Lola's brother, he is also revealed to be interested in this fellow man. However, the social environment and norms this teen is in, expect him to suppress such feelings, and to live as an individual in parallel with his social sexuality and according to social norms, without allowing him to act instinctively.

Spots in the film seem to have some certain representations. Where the racist, homophobic and transphobic German teens beat Murat with racist, homophobic and transphobic hate speeches, is Olympiastadion, which was built in 1936, when fascism was on the rise. Also, that Berlin Victory Column, which is shown in the final scene of the film, is next to Tiergarten, where LGBT individuals "search for companions", and that the Sexology Institute of Magnus Hirschfeld was founded here, indicates how strong Ataman's selection of spot is and a gradually developing gay culture in Berlin (Safoğlu, 2008b:46-47; Baird, 2004:63).

## IN LIEU OF CONCLUSION: LESBIAN (L), GAY (G), BISEXUAL (B), TRANSSEXUAL (T), TRANSVESTITE (T), INTERSEXUAL (I), QUEER (Q)

In our daily lives, we do not recognise that even a survey question imposes social sexuality rather than a sexual identity. However, even such small codes disallow individuals to reveal their sexual identity, and may oppress the individual, provides two options only.

As the social perspective is shaped around biological sex, which is "binary", the problem of LGBT existence in the language, has led to the emergence of a conflict between representation and reality in the cinema as

---

1 http://www.dw.de/e%C5%9Fcinsel-evlilik-10-ya%C5%9F%C4%B1nda/a-15278792.

text. Constant reconstruction of society due to changes and evolutions during different periods has had a reflection in the cinematic discourse, which actually acts a mirror. Studies on LGBT individuals, and the professionals stating that such individuals are not sick, perverts or heretics, and especially the emergence of independent cinema in the 90s led to some evolution in the representation of LGBT characters. Both Turkish cinema and European and American cinema went through this evolution and with Stonewall Riots in 1969, the resistance by LGBT individuals also had a positive impression. The representation of reality has become a milestone in terms of proving their existence in the public and revealing that LGBT is real. A scenario that is shaped around a director's ideology and ideas attempts to convince the audience that what is shown and said is true. This, when considered in the context of queer cinema, may either lead to prejudice against LGBT individuals and stronger stereotypes or may lead to destruction of heteronormative judgements.

Representations such as "Lola and Billy The Kid", which do not breach the boundaries of reality may not be complying with the circumstances of their period, however, they may preserve their nature as masterpieces and allow analysis in later periods, as they address may sociological concepts. Therefore, Ataman's choice on Berlin when picturing LGBT identity within the context of Turkish diaspora in Germany, is not a coincidence. The film, with the synthesis of immigrant and homosexual and the wig, becoming a symbol that manufactures a meaning, not only challenge the codes of heteronormativity, but also presented as an indicator and representation of sexual identity both in Ataman's book "Peruk Takan Kadınlar", and in the film "Lola and Billy The Kid".

In the film, the Turks as immigrants, who are alienated due to their religious, linguistic and racial differences, are employed as unskilled labours and therefore are forced to use their sexual identities to earn their lives. They make their lives by trading their lives illegally in certain public places, where gay subculture is established (public toilets, night clubs etc.). In this respect, the film also reveals how immigrant Turkish LGBT are commodified in entertainment market, with all its realities.

It is clearly seen that homosexual individuals may also be homophobic, and their speech may be based on the concept of "masculinity", due to their belonging to a heterosexist society. That is why Bili wants Lola to change sex and become a female, and a "housewife" as Turkish society and heteronormativity require, which would save him from being called a "fairy". That is, he tries to create a binary sexual stereotype out of his partner, as he is unable to change the stereotypes.

Lola, being killed by his brother due to his transgender identity, is a representation of the "others" victimised by hate crimes, which are mostly made look like an accident. That the film reproduces the social realities through representations such as class, sex, subject and identity, and making them a part of a certain context, are important in terms of the indicators presented to the audience.

Cinema will function properly through the presentation of inartificial truths to the society and by means of films produced on liberal platforms, which are not oppressed by the power mechanisms. This is the only way, which LGBT individuals will be represented correctly in daytime cinema, without being an element of humour and commodified.

# REFERENCES

Abisel, N. (1999) *Popüler Sinema ve Türler.* İstanbul: Alan.

Agacinski, S. (1998). *Cinsiyetler Siyaseti,* Ankara: Dost Kitabevi.

Alam, M. (2009) "Kutluğ Ataman: Esas Oyuncu Atmosferdir", http://www.mafm.boun.edu.tr/files/63_KutluğAtaman.pdf, Accessed: 04.08.2013.

Ataman, K. (2001). *Peruk Takan Kadınlar.* İstanbul: Metis.

Avcı, P. (2013) "Teslimiyet ve Türk Sinemasında Farklı Cinsel Yaşantılar 1", http://www.kaosgl.com/sayfa.php?id=6036, Accessed: 04.08.2013.

Baird, V. (2004) Cinsel Çeşitlilik-Yönelimler Politikalar Haklar ve İhlaller, İstanbul: Metis.

Baykal, E. (2008) "Beşinci Karenin Gösterdiği: Öznelden Toplumsal Kimliğin Portresine", *Kutluğ Ataman: Sen Zaten Kendini Anlat!.* İstanbul: Yapı Kredi.

Benshoff H. & Griffin S. (2004) "General Introduction: Queer Cinema, Film Reader", *Queer Cinema: The Film Reader,* NY: Routledge.

Carmona, C. R. (2016) "Cinema and It's Ability to Represent a Staged Reality", http://doc.ubi.pt/19/artigos_7.pdf, Accessed: 28.06.2018.

Davies, S. P. (2010) Eşcinsel Sineması Tarihi: Sinemada Görünür Olmak, İstanbul: Kalkedon.

Diken, B. & Laustsen C. B. (2011) *Filmlerle Sosyoloji,* İstanbul: Metis.

DW, (2011) "Eşcinsel Evlilik 10 Yaşında" http://www.dw.de/e%C5%9Fcinsel-evlilik-10-ya%C5%9F%C4%B1nda/a-15278792, Accessed: 12.07.2013.

Farago, F. (2011) *Sanat,* Ankara: Doğubatı.

Gezgin, M. F. (2013) "Cemaat-Cemiyet Ayrımı ve Ferdinand Tönnies", http://www.journals.istanbul.edu.tr/tr/index.php/iktisatsosyoloji/article/download/6356/5880, Accessed: 22.07.2013.

Hok, H. & Leung, S. (2004) "New Queer Cinema and Third Cinema", *New Queer Cinema: A Critical Reader,* der. Michele Aaron, USA: Rutgers University.

İri, M. (2011). Sinema Araştırmaları: Kuramlar, Kavramlar, Yaklaşımlar, İstanbul: Derin.

Jones, D.M. & Juett, J.C. (2010) *Coming Out to the Mainstream: New Queer Cinema in he 21st Century.* Newcastle upon Tyne: Cambridge Scholars.

Kabadayı, L. (2013) Film Eleştirisi: Kuramsal Çerçeve ve Sinemamızdan Örnek Çözümlemeler. İstanbul: Ayrıntı.

Koç, D. (2008). Feminist Sinema ve Film Teorisi. İstanbul: Agora.

Öğüt H. & Z. Deniz (2012) "Geçmişten Günümüze Türkiye Sinemasında LGBT Temsilleri", *20. LGBT Onur Haftası Bildiri Kitabı-BELLEK,* İstanbul.

Özgüç, A. (2000) *Türk Sinemasında Cinselliğin Tarihi.* İstanbul: Parantez.

Pullen, C. (2012) "Queer art of parallaxed document: The visual discourse of docudrag in Kutlug Ataman's Never My Soul!", *LGBT Transnational Identity and the Media.* London: Palgrave Macmillan.

Rich, B. R. (1995) *Homo Pomo: The New Queer Cinema,* ed. Pam Cook ve Philip Dodd Londra: Scarlet.

_____ (2013) *New Queer Cinema: The Director's Cut,* http://www.jstor.org/stable/10.1525/

fq.2013.67.1.89, Accessed: 07.07.2018.

Safoğlu, A. (2008a) "Ortalığa (S)açılmış 100 Film", *KAOS GL Dergi*, May-June, Issue 100.

_____ (2008b) "Zamir Meloş'un Gölgesindekiler", *KAOS GL Dergi,* November-December, Issue 103.

Selek, P. (2011) *Maskeler Süvariler Gacılar.* Ankara: Ayizi.

Tuna, M. & Özbek, Ç. (2012) *Yerlileşen Yabancılar: Güney Ege Bölgesi'nde Göç, Yurttaşlık ve Kimliğin Dönüşümü.* Ankara: Detay.

Ulusay, N. (2011) "Yeni Queer Sinema: Öncesi ve Sonrası", Fe Dergi 3, No 1.

Wolf, S. (2012) *Cinsellik ve Sosyalizm: LGBT Özgürleşmesinin Tarihi, Politikası ve Teorisi,* İstanbul: Sel.

Yamaner, G. (2009) "Sanatta Homofobik ve Cinsiyetçi Dil ve Göstergelerin Kurulumu", *Uluslararası Homofobi Karşıtı Buluşma Bildiri Kitabı,* Ankara.

# CHAPTER 8

# KAOS GL MAGAZINE'S ROLE IN THE EMERGENCE OF THE LGBTI PUBLIC SPHERE IN TURKEY[1]

İdil Engindeniz

Jürgen Habermas' work entitled "The Structural Transformation of the Public Sphere. An Inquiry into a Category of Bourgeois Society" has brought the concept of "public sphere" to an important place in social science debates, since its publication in German in 1962, but especially in 1989 when it was translated into English. Since then Habermas has been criticized by feminist readings and counter-public sphere approaches, and Habermas himself has made several changes in his approach over time. In France in 2010, Professor on sciences of information and communication, Bernard Miège's "L'espace public contemporain. Approche info-communicationnelle" (Contemporary public sphere, informational-communicative approach) also introduced a new approach and proceeded through the concept of "societal public sphere". The challenge is to show how the concept of public sphere, which is used in the field of political science, can also be useful in terms of communication sciences, as well as allowing us to evaluate different public spheres which can include not only rational discussion, but also personal narratives. To answer if another structural form of public sphere can be possible, we will try to find whether the magazine Kaos GL has created an LGBTI public sphere through content and discourse analysis methods since 1994, when it was being published for the first time. Besides the basic features of the public sphere, we also take into account the approach put forward by Miège. For this purpose, the sections of the magazine entitled "Postcards from Life", "Letters of Literature", "Testimonies" were analyzed because of being the parts that can contribute to the emergence of a possible public sphere via the magazine. We examine what kind of discourse on violence is created through "Testimonies" and how the debate about the "gay movement" has been

---

[1] This article is derived from a doctoral dissertation entitled "L'émergence d'un espace public LGBTI en Turquie: l'analyse de la revue Kaos GL", advocated at the University of Grenoble in 2012.

115

conducted from the discussions put forward by the magazine (or by the readers). This study was realized by the analysis of 105 issues of the magazine (covering the period of September 1994-March / April 2009) and it aims to reveal the clues about the construction of an LGBTI public sphere in Turkey during a period when different public spheres approaches were not known and while the persons who participated to its emergence had certainly not naming what they do such as an emergence of public sphere. One of the main lines to follow while doing this will be to ask if this eventual public sphere has an alternative character, what is its attitudes towards the mainstream discourses, what is the nature of the relationships established with other counter-public spheres of the society. Another aim of the work is also to expose the importance of the publications that have as audience a specific group (a minority), especially during the period of the construction of their own identity and with their ability to permit to its members to express themselves, to make hear their own voices, even if it seems that they have less influence comparing to the mass media.

As we have already seen in our PhD thesis (Engindeniz Şahan, 2012), when we look at the discourse produced by the Kaos GL via the magazine and about different topics, we observe that the group has at the first place a firmer approach but does not reject the possibilities of dialogue and with time, it cooperates with other actors in the fields of its priorities.

Another distinctive feature of the group is that it does not limit the target mass to a group that shares only similar features / problems / distresses, but also attempts to transform the antagonistic actors. The group does not do this only through publications, it tries to establish a relationship and make a sphere for itself by existing in the field. Thus, over time, we see that the group has been accepted as "an actor" and was taken "seriously", henceforth it was invited for different collaborations (meetings, lectures, etc.) by universities and by other institutions.

In the context of our work we will briefly talk about what is the public sphere in its classical sense. According to Habermas, the public sphere emerged in a certain period of history and in certain geographies, and even searching for the existence of the public sphere outside these times and places does not constitute a very meaningful work. Habermas' public sphere existed between the 17th-19th centuries and emerged in England, France and Germany. It is a bourgeois public sphere based on rational debate and aims a consensus. One basic characteristic of that public sphere is that it is a political sphere, in the strict sense of politics, while we were not talking about "what is private is political". According to Habermas, the public sphere is formed after various discussions, the collision of different ideas, the "exchange of logical arguments", and it is always expected that a settlement (a consensus) will be reached as a result of these discussions (Girod, 2000: p. 26).

The date of the emergence of the public sphere coincides with the urbanization and with the emergence of the concept of the private sphere within the bourgeoisie. Other factors that effected the emergence of the public sphere were the decreased importance of agriculture and the development of the commerce. These changes bring about the change of the economic system and also of the social structure. The beginning of change of private and public concepts is decisive in the formation of public sphere. For example, the Church gradually becomes a private sphere. Later on, this time, topics that are considered private until that time will start going out to the public sphere and it will be witnessed again that the public sphere has changed. Habermas shows how the meetings in the "salons" and cafes contribute to the proliferation of political (and other) debates, and these discussions are also gain publicity via the media of the period (opinion press).

Hans Verstraeten, professor in the field of communications, summarizes the elements of Habermas' public sphere (1996, 348):

1) The public sphere requires a 'forum' that is accessible to as many people as possible and where a large variety of social experiences can be expressed and exchanged.
2) In the public sphere, the various arguments and views are confronted through rational discussion. This implies that 'rational' political choice is possible only if the public sphere first offers a clear insight into the possible alternatives from which one can choose. At the same time, the media should offer the widest possible range of interpretation frames so that the citizen is also aware of what he did not choose (Murdock, 1992: 17-41).
3) Systematically and critically checking on government policies is the primary task for this public sphere.

Some of the criticisms directed at Habermas focus on the glorification of rationality, and the exclusion of other methods of self-expression because of being valueless. Another criticism, first expressed by Nancy Fraser, is that this public sphere is too masculine, and that women do not exist in this area. However, some subsequent research reveals that women are not so erased from the public domain in the period in question. Another area that lacks on this sphere is the proletariat. Habermas acknowledges this criticism and states that he refers to the proletariat in the public sphere, but mainly works about the bourgeois public sphere. Another criticism is that the public sphere is treated as if there is an absolute equality in that sphere.

Another approach to addressing the relationship between the public sphere and the media was developed by Bernard Miège. Miège defines the public sphere as a place where communicative actions take place, and historically it is shaped by four different forms of communication (2010: p. 116). What determines these forms is the dominant communication technologies at the time. Accordingly, there are periods when the following models dominate:

- Opinion journalism
- Mainstream media / commercialized press
- Audiovisual media
- Generalized public relations

At the point where we come today, Miège describes the public sphere as the various places and moments in which all kinds of public and private questions are spoken rationally but also emotionally. In other words, that solid rational approach in Habermas, the usage of the language at a certain level, softens; the concept of a public sphere not very political in the classical way, and more societal emerges from personal stories.

In our research, we examined the Kaos GL magazine, which has been published since 1994, on the basis of the following question: Is it possible to create a LGBTI public sphere through the magazine? Being the first publication addressing directly to LGBTI community, the magazine deserves a much more in-depth and separate study, but because of the limits of our research we examined firstly the general lines of the magazine, and then we looked at more specific issues which seem important to the formation of the LGBTI public sphere (the topics discussed, the personal stories that permit a foundation of an "LGBTI" discourse, etc.).

## Establishment process of Kaos GL Magazine

The formation of the group and the launch of the magazine parallel to this are reported on the website of Kaos GL Association as following:

*"At the beginning of the 1990's we were chatting at home. Sometimes we wanted to organize 'gay pride' with the news we read from the newspapers. Sometimes our morale was deteriorating, 'nothing can be done in this country', we were leaving our dreams..."[2]*

About the purpose of a publication, it is said in the same article, "We had to touch every individual's hand, we had to enter every house. We could do this only by publishing a magazine". In 1993, the publication project began to become more concrete with debates on possible forms of that eventual publication. From the beginning, it is expressed that they are not interested in being limited to a single city, they want to expand and to share their desire to fight discrimination that concerns them. Firstly, another publication is used to reach other LGBTIs: the weekly Express magazine that the slogan is "not the voice of its owner, its own voice". We see that the call of the group was published on the twelfth issue of the magazine on April 16-23, 1994. This call attracts attention as it is addressed not only to male and female homosexuals but also to whom are against heterosexism. This shows us that

---

[2] http://www.kaosgldernegi.org/belge.php?id=tarihce

the oppositional positioning to heterosexism, which is underlined to illustrate that LGBTI rights do not merely concern only LGBTIs today, exists even when the group is still in the process of establishing itself. It also shows us the base on which Kaos GL, one of the most important components of the LGBTI movement, grown. It was underlined that homosexuals were in fact all over the society, but that they had to live under an identity imposed by heterosexism. It is mentioned that the time for changing these imposed identities is coming up, and it is mentioned that a mail box has been taken in this way to create a communication network and to bring together those who want to walk together later. The call invites the readers to write about their own problems, their feelings and also how they can contribute, and ends with a question: "Who else can we trust, if we cannot trust ourselves?". However, although a kind of opening and trusting call is being made for homosexuals, we can say that the callers, at least in that first stage, are having trouble with this, because there is no clear name or address on the call, and the communication has to be made through a mail box that offers anonymity is expected to occur. A similar trend will also be seen in the first issues of the magazine, and the writings will usually be published with pseudonyms, not with the real names of the authors. It is difficult to say that, even there has been positive progress in denying visibility in the past years, even today it is not a subject achieved completely.

Kaos GL, first published in September 1994, identifies itself as an "underground" publication in technical and spiritual dimensions[3]. At the 25th issue of the magazine (September 1996), a letter signed by Atilla Karakış tells us the emergence of the idea of the magazine and the publication process of the magazine:

*"We had lot of things to tell, we wouldn't have problem about finding writings. But we wanted everyone to hear our voice. We wanted all homosexuals and anti-heterosexist heterosexuals to write without having 'what to write', 'how to write' anxiety. We had enough from the writings, from the so-called researches that had no idea about us, that supposedly understood us. All the magazines, Aktüel, Tempo Nokta or another one, the homosexuality has been covered many times; there was nothing left, except pages that did not tell anything or words that made plain ridicule. Yeah, now it's our time, the time of homosexuals. The time to exist in our own magazine, with our own expressions ... If there was no computer under our hand, we would have typed our scripts secretly at our work places. If we had no money for the printing press, we would duplicate the magazine by photocopy. We did not know the mass that our magazine would reach, literally, our language was heavy. We did not know the market; the copy was under the quality we wanted. We did not know how to use a computer; our page layout was inefficient. But despite all these and the negativities outside, KAOS born*

---

[3] From the interview made by a fanzin called Cyberpunk and published in İzmir. The interview is published also on Kaos GL magazine, 11th issue (July 1995, p. 16).

on 20 September 1994."

In the 67th issue, we observe the idea of creating a special sphere for LGBTIs, via the article entitled "What's new in Kaos". Murat Yalçınkaya, who signed the article, defines the journal by asking a rhetorical question:

*"Kaos GL magazine set out to create an area for the LGBTIs from Turkey where they can tell their own words, is not one of the centers to build an oppositional discourse?"*

In 2002, issue 74, another idea that is complementary to this idea is being put forward: make visible the homosexuality by supporting the struggle for homosexuals' liberation and create their own agenda. In the 84th issue of July-August 2004, this time Umut Güner stated in the editorial that they aim with the Kaos GL Magazine to create a magazine where the homosexuals who cannot express themselves outside / anywhere, can make hear their own voices.

As Atilla Karakış and other members expressed in various ways, the first years of the magazine passed with lack of technical possibilities and with financial difficulties. The magazine is published with a professional printing only from its 40th issue published in December 1997. It has been indicated that this change is not because of the improved financial state of the group but because of the requirement of working with a professional distribution company. Due to the accumulation of the distribution channels in the hands of certain large groups, the distribution is a problem for every alternative publication in Turkey, this is why the new delivery system could work only for a short time.

The group communicates with its readers via mail for a long period of time. Since the group does not have a fixed place, the sending of the letters is done through a mailbox which is first anonymous and then opened on behalf of Ali Özbaş. Since joining The International Lesbian, Gay, Bisexual, Trans and Intersex Association (ILGA) in January 1997, the group now has an e-mail address given to them by ILGA (kaosgl @ ilga.org). Nevertheless, in January 1998, in the 40th issue of the magazine we observe a call inviting the readers to send their letters with a more readable hand-writing. This gives a clue that electronic mail has still not been used a lot by the readership. In April 1999 (issue 56), the mail address of the group changed (kaosgl@geocities.com). When we came to April 1999 (issue 61), we can see that Ali Özbaş's e-mail address is used for contact in the event of a solidarity dinner.

Electronic mail, appeared in parallel with the development of internet in Turkey in the 2000s, becomes increasingly a more frequently admitted way to communicate for the magazine. In the 67th issue of August-September 2000 period, Murat Yalçınkaya pointed out that apart from the postal address and phone numbers, the group has an important mailing list (group) with the aim of facilitating the communication of the members during the preparation of the magazine, and invites readers who want to contribute to Kaos GL to be a member of that mailing list (group). A year later, in summer 2001 (issue 70), the group announces the change of fax numbers, but adds that after the electronic mail has been switched on, almost no other communication means are used. This form of communication (new for the period) has an important feature in terms of LGBTIs: facilitating access to the group by reducing the danger of unwanted visibility. In the fifty-fourth issue, a reader named Çiğdem states that she cannot attend the Kaos GL meetings because she lives far from Ankara. After adding the fact that she cannot subscribe to the magazine because her environment is not suitable, she says that thanks to the technology she can follow up the group from the internet and can contact the group via its e-mail address: "Long live the technology!".

The article published in the first issue, entitled "Current Situation and Homosexuality", gives us some clues on topics to be discussed in the future: medicine, psychiatry, genetic engineering, class society, school and family. The genetic engineering is criticized because of its tries to find the "cause of homosexuality"; class society because it empowers the capitalism and the male domination; the school and the family are criticized for imposing a heterosexual socialization on young LGBTIs. The article ends with the determination that individual effort is not enough to change heterosexual socialization and that LGBTIs need to organize to achieve this goal. This is an important point in terms of the construction of the discourse on the subject of "violence" to be mentioned in the following paragraphs.

In the first issue of the magazine, the text which is published as a kind of manifesto and which informs the establishment of the magazine is written in all capital letters. In terms of the rules of conduct on the Internet (netiquette), it refers to scream and anger. Even if internet was not on a common usage at the time of the publication of the magazine, we can argue that the usage of the capital letters indicates also an anger, a rage. The group's anger appears to be against the existing system, the texts indicates that same as women who are oppressed just because of being women, "the heterosexist mentality and its patriarchal structure" targets also the destruction of homosexuals. At this point the group likens homosexuals to American Indians, Jews, and Kurds (this is the first time Kaos GL talks about this important subject in Turkey). These sentences show us that the group places itself and thus the LGBTI movement, in an equal survival struggle with peoples and ethnic groups that are mass-massacred.

Likewise, the title of a second article published by Ediz Öztürk under the heading "Unite all the homosexuals of the world" refers to the famous statement of the Communist Manifesto. The article also refers to the need to come together to fight discrimination against homosexuals, such as the organization of "workers, grocery and women".

When it is thought about a societal public sphere's interest in politics and if it can be also an opposing public sphere, these references observed in the magazine and one of the answers to the questions submitted to the magazine in its third issue enlightens us about that eventuality.

*"Kaos GL is political? Is it possible that something else happens? (...) In the strict sense of political Kaos GL is not political! I mean, it has no connection with parliament or with government. It has no aim to come to power, nor wants the heterosexual masculine power. (...) Kaos GL rejects all categories of power defined by heterosexual masculine power: and it must be accepted that this is political. Not being just at the level of rejection of all given categories, but at the same time, trying and struggling for the purpose of creating an identity as gay and lesbian, it is something politic. There is nothing to complain about, Kaos GL is political in this sense."*

## Language of the magazine

Although the pages of the Kaos GL magazine are open to everyone, the language of the magazine itself is criticized for being incomprehensible to its readers. In the third issue of the magazine (November 1996), the group says that they are taking serious the critics about the language because the magazine is a "communication tool" but that there is nothing to do. The group askes readers to make a little more effort to understand, says also that another possible solution to such a problem is the proliferation of publications addressing different segments. However, it is possible to observe in the other articles that the group itself uses a more informal language, so it can be argued that the magazine is not merely aimed at reaching "educated" homosexuals, and that linguistic coercion is somewhat because of the utilization of some concepts new at that period. As a matter of fact, a discussion is being made on how to name homosexuals and homosexuality even in the later issue of the magazine (e.g. April-May 2003, issue 77). In this sense, it would not be wrong to say that language is one of the key areas of struggle for LGBTI movement. Discussions on naming continue three more times, not just homosexuals, but also linguists and translators are invited to discuss. It is said that the emergence of new terms creates a kind of chaos environment (Kaos GL magazine, March-April 2005), saying that "if we want to create a new language other than the heterosexual and masculine one, we have to have our common points". This underscores the need to create a common language so that discussions can move forward well, although people are allowed to express themselves as they wish. While a homosexual societal public sphere is being created, a language that makes it possible is also being created.

## Violence

Before looking at what kind of rhetoric was produced in Kaos GL Magazine through physical violence towards all homosexuals it would be appropriate to mention some of the practices that homosexuals face on the socialization places. Even if they are maintaining some of their validity, especially based on the mid-90's when the LGBTI movement began to emerge on these lands, we can count among the socialization places of homosexuals, parks, cinemas and Turkish baths. As far as we understand from the letters sent to the magazine, the mentioned places can be found in almost every city and are known by the homosexuals. These venues are the occasion for LGBTIs to meet each other and provide a place to make a rupture with the sense of loneliness. Although one of the main aims of the frequentation of these places is to find partners, friendships can be developed and experience transfer is provided. These places are not out of danger, there are hazards such as being humiliated by the police, being tortured and being taken into custody, as well as the ill-treatment of people who come to the parks to be with LGBTI people but who do not define themselves as LGBTI. In this environment, one sees that not only him, but also other homosexuals, are exposed to similar treatment, and the discrimination in the physical places allows that the "consciousness of being different" becomes more concrete. Together with others who are subjected to the same discrimination, there is a likelihood that a temporary or permanent solidarity. In this sense, it can be argued that physical places contribute to the formation of identity consciousness.

Physical violence in the above-mentioned places is a factor that feeds another discourse in Kaos GL magazine. The early issues of the magazine warn homosexuals to be cautious, and it is stated that if they are tackled together, problems can be solved more easily. The concrete problems encountered in everyday life are used to provide solidarity and to build solidarity over the fighting issues.

From the very first issue of the magazine, LGBTI persons are informed about the possible attacks they may come in and are told their rights against the police, and are advised to be cautious about the police. The magazine underscores the need for homosexuals to come and defend themselves, and this first call corresponds to a very physical defense, suggesting the establishment of "self-defense units". Then readers are invited to write about their testimonies of the violence they are subjected to, and the title "Testimonies" is created in the magazine. In this way, from a problem that is experienced by almost all homosexuals is provided, firstly the possibility for people to express themselves, to make themselves visible (even with aliases), and then try to create a discourse about legal mechanisms of violence and system.

Between the first and 85th issue of the magazine, 27 testimonies are published, two letters published under this heading reveal the homophobia that one of the readers/writers. This disclosure is important to note that the person who exposed to homophobia, takes a certain power from the magazine Kaos GL, against the other person. The person says that "I will send your writings (to the magazine), and this aggressive stance will not be hidden". During the interviews conducted for the PhD thesis, which constituted the basis of the study, a male homosexual also stated that he had formed a similar sentence was organized and did not feel lonely in the face of any discriminatory movement that he is now in because he was aware of the organizations. Even if a person is not an active part, knowing the existence of a homosexual movement ensures that one feels more secure in public spheres.

If we turn to violence again; again under the heading of "Testimonies", there are also group writings, sometimes written in the name of the group, sometimes written in the name of one of the members. For example, the first issue of the similarity of police violence in Palestine and in Turkey, it is mentioned that this is not surprising. These writings on violence begin to lose some of their continuity with the 85th issue of "violence". However, in the meantime, the consciousness of the existence and causes of "violence against homosexuals" has been raised by going out of the individual stories of the persons and allowed people to express themselves in the way they want; discussions about the ways of struggle against the violence that they are facing because of their identity and independently from their singular stories. We can argue that construction of a discourse based on singular stories but which goes beyond them to arrive to a coherent discourse including all of them, this is one of the embodied forms of the approach that we call "societal public sphere" in the sense of allowing both the private and the collective.

### "What kind of gay movement"

One of the main discussions carried out in the magazine is the "What kind of gay movement" debate. From our hypothesis about an eventual societal public sphere built around the Kaos GL magazine, we examined this debate in response to the following questions:

• Is the participation of the persons encouraged by the founders of the magazine?

• Does it really the participation of different people is in question or is it monopolized by a few people?

• How do discussions work? Does it develop in response to previous articles, or is it about to express different ideas without a debate or without an endeavor to create a coherence in the whole?

• What language is being used and does it give us a clue about the status of interpersonal relationships?

Since its second issue, Kaos GL begins publishing texts until its 21th issue of May 1996 that will form the basis of the debate that will going on under the title of "gay movement". For two years, in a national and global context, a basis for discussion is created through writings that will help settle homosexuality on a historical level.

Yeşim Başaran, in the twenty-first issue, invites other people to join her and starts a debate about how the gay movement should be, and this debate lasts a little over a year, until June 97. Twenty-four articles will be published by seventeen different people within the scope of the discussion. In the first article, she poses a fundamental question about the differentiation of the homosexual movement from simple legal demands and questions the gap between politics and the homosexual movement. The author asks if the only two concerns of the movement are the improvement of the laws concerning discrimination experienced by homosexuals and the fight to make them accept the presence of these in the legislative texts. Başaran emphasizes the fact that the absence of laws that prohibit or penalize homosexuality are also part of a certain strategy and show in a certain way ignorance about homosexuality: by not naming it, one can more easily deny its existence. Yet she insists on the reflections of the presence or absence of laws in the daily lives of homosexual individuals living in a society. She criticizes the whole system that forces every individual to live according to the established norms in order to survive. She indicates that sometimes, in order to live in society, especially when it comes to minorities, some sacrifice is demanded and that results the destruction of personal identity. Accordingly, she adds that this fact makes easier to distinguish the absurdity and impossibility of the system, especially for minorities, due to their direct exposure to negative parts of the order. She questions the legitimacy search of homosexuals in a world built on and based on a heterosexual system. This system also includes media: the writer says that it is not meaningful to demand a no-homophobic approach from the media to homosexuals:

*"What can expect homosexuals from the media who are instruments to chain the brains and to reproduce enslaved minds every day? (...) Thinking the visual media as a serious way of communication is a terrible misconception, it means not seeing the media's association with the stinking system, and / or not disturbed by the system."*

This first article shows us the general lines of the emerging LGBTI movement in Turkey once again. First, a general critique of the established system is targeted, so criticism of the identity politics, especially attributed to new social movements, begins to lose weight in this instance. There is a movement that is not isolated on a single problem (of LGBTIs), the movement is trying to link this particular problem to the general system. This feature of the LGBTI movement in Turkey emerge as an important element. At this point, if the others agree, it will open up the common action with different movements. Secondly, through the writings we learn that movement is looking for alternative ways of communication. With the publication of Kaos GL magazine, it will be possible for homosexuals to speak at their own pace rather than seeking a place for themselves in other publications. Over the years, the relationship established by the group with the media has changed drastically, but the importance given to having an own publication of LGBTIs will not change.

Table 1: Names and texts contributing to the discussion on homosexual movement.

| Issue | Date | Contribution |
|---|---|---|
| 21 | May 1996 | Yeşim Başaran |
| 24 | August 1996 | Batur Özdinç: About the freedom of gays Yasemin Özalp Barış Evren: My ideas about the discussion on what kind of gay movement Can Atak – Burak Cem Evrim: Ideas about gay and lesbian movement Kemal Yigit: Being different, but... Hasan: An essay about "gay culture" in Turkey |
| 25 | September 1996 | Emil: Ideas, impressions, references, sarcasm Sedat: What kind of discussion about the gay movement Devrim: Ideas about gay and lesbian movement |
| 26 | October 1996 | Yeşim Başaran Gay'e Efendisiz |
| 27 | November 1996 | Cengiz: The emergence of gay culture Atilla A. Mehmet |
| 29 | January 1997 | Gay'e Efendisiz: New social movements |
| 30 | February 1997 | Yeşim T. Başaran: Lesbians, we will now eat Luna? |
| 31 | March 1997 | Bora |
| 32 | April 1997 | Atilla A. Cengiz: Gay identity Yasemin Özalp |
| 34 | June 1997 | Halil Seyhan |

After Başaran's first writing, the discussion proceeds in two different planes: some sent letters are answering the previously published letters and develop the subject; other writings contribute to the debate by addressing the issue from different angles. Therefore, it is not easy to find an uninterrupted line of functioning of the debate, but it is not regarded as a defect by the movement's forerunners, it is treated as a contribution to the development of the movement and it is not attempted to "correct" such contributions in order to "fit to the rules of discussion".

Although there are a large number of people involved in the debate, we will see in the article of Batur Özdinç an answer about why this number is not higher:

*"When I said my manuscript appeared in the Kaos GL magazine, the first reaction was to ask if I was gay."*

If we consider that being open is a multi-layered subject, be open to family, to friends, in business place and so on, it would not be wrong to argue that the possibility of such labeling by the entourage can have a negative effect on LGBTIs to write to the magazine, to participate to the debate.

Again, in the twenty-fourth issue, Yasemin Özalp mentions the importance of organizing, that the structure of that organization is not important at all, that it is possible to do everything but a political party. Özalp, who does not elaborate this opposition, discusses the general lines that she predicts for the LGBTI movement. It is also a general criticism of society:

*"I think that homosexuals should question institutions such as the family, the state, religion, education, the media, and should aim for a social structure that is not based on destruction and ignorance."*

Özalp invites homosexuals to collaborate with civil society organizations, trade unions, independent media organs and individuals, while leading a serious criticism of such institutions. This invitation is also important in that it shows once again that the homosexual movement is not considered separate from other components of society.

In the third article of the twenty-fourth issue, Barış Evren, underlines the importance of getting together under one single group instead of creating many small groups. Evren states that the existence of different ideas within a single large group is always possible and that such a group is more effective than small groups of ten. Evren himself is a concrete example of such a disagreement: he indicates that he does not share the ideas of Kaos GL and he also underscores that he is not agree neither with Yeşim Başaran. Unlike Başaran, Evren advocates that certain laws that guarantee the rights of homosexuals should come into force and question what is foreseen as a means of struggle if it is not intended to achieve certain legal rights:

*"Are we going to demonstrate in the streets? Or will we meet once a month, once a week, to destroy the state? What are we going to get without laws, without initiatives before the Parliament?"*

One of the critics of Evren is about Kaos GL's policy towards the media.

By excluding the media, he claims that Kaos GL has lost the ability to make heard his own voice, to reach out to other homosexuals who have no idea neither about the group nor the magazine. Evren suggests to try to transform the media and use them consciously. Kaos GL's policy towards the media will undergo a change in this direction over the years. In the first issues of the magazine, the angrier, sharper discourse is dominant and the media takes its share from this discourse. Nowadays, although the approach towards the media is more inclusive and transformative, in its first period the group considers the media as part of the system against which must lead a struggle. It would be wrong to explain this change by saying that the LGBTI movement is now a part of the system. Our argument is that this change is related to the maturation of the movement and to the different actors it faces, by their ability to develop different struggle techniques. Various people who have been in movement for many years say that even negative publications in the mainstream media can be regarded as a field gained in terms of visibility.

The debate about how the homosexual movement should take place lasts about a year with the various contributions of different people and ends in June 1997. Although there are various writings in the proceeding numbers on the subject, the discussion will not continue in a structured way on the magazine pages.

## Conclusion

One of the main questions that emerged at the beginning of our doctoral dissertation was to show how the concepts of "civil society" and "public sphere" in a non-European geographical region correspond to a reality. Previously conducted studies about the meaning of these concepts in a no-European geography helped us and, in our research, we also tried to follow their leads; we tried to show what are the meanings of these concepts from Ottoman Empire to actual Turkey. Undoubtedly, concepts arise from social realities, and each society has its own specificities about these realities. It will be difficult to find concepts that can apply equally to all societies. However, this difficulty does not mean that the mentioned concepts do not exist in those societies. Our work has shown us that there are various difficulties in trying to understand the light of the concepts developed in Europe outside the European societies. However, these concepts have also shown that the concepts of civil society and public sphere in our work, in particular, can take different forms in different geographies.

Another factor that makes us think throughout our work is the legitimacy of the word: who does speak for whom and what gives it a legitimacy? These questions are already embodied: if the Kurds' rights are defended by a Turk, is this more legitimate? Is not there a hierarchy between different parts of the society in this case? If the person who speaks about LGBTIs is a heterosexual, or if the parents are involved in this process, is this not a more acceptable framework for society? Who has to talk in this case? At which point is this a communicative tactic, at which point is it a process that reproduces the stereotypes and system? So what can be the ways in which the minorities express themselves? etc.

These questions are at the same time related about our hypothesis on the skeptical character of the civil society and of the public sphere in Turkey. Because of the ideological distinction between the "Islamists" and "nationalists" and those who do not want to be part of one of these two groups, the discourses expressed are never accepted as they are, hidden meanings are always sought. It is therefore almost impossible to establish the sound foundations necessary to maintain a rational discussion on any issue. In such an environment, after the examination of Kaos GL Magazine from various angles, it may be possible to say that the magazine created the conditions for a kind of public sphere. We can see that in Kaos GL magazine one of the criteria that existed in Habermas's thought was realized: all the social conditions (class conditions) are forgotten in these areas, people, as "ordinary" individuals are independent from every hierarchy they can reveal themselves (Taner, 2008: 49). It can be said that any kind of "isolation from social conditions" principle is fulfilled in public sphere created through magazine. In theory and in practice up to a certain level, we can claim that there is such an openness in the contribution to the magazine. But is there not a hierarchy between people, even with the level of language used? Expressing their own feelings or personal experiences on a much more casual level in front of the participants using the "ostentatious" words; those who cannot argue their ideas as they need to, will they lack courage for their next participation? The, positive, answers to these questions being hidden in themselves, they do not show us the whole picture yet because even if there is the possibility of domination of "well educated" LGBTIs on the political decision-making process by the "natural" exclusion of others, there are always "new comers" who discover the group, the magazine, the internet site and who are not familiar to these established codes, if they exist, so a less refined sound will never disappear, and will allow the movement to reach a wider audience, rather than being held to believe that the movement is limited in a little group with a perfect consistency.

## REFERENCES

Engindeniz Şahan, İ. (2012) L'émergence d'un espace public LGBTI en Turquie: l'analyse de la revue Kaos GL, not published PhD thesis: Université Grenoble.

Girod, A., (2000) Les mutations de l'espace public et la construction médiatique de 'l'opinion publique', not published PhD thesis: Lyon 2.

Kaos GL Magazine, Issues 1-105, September 1994 – March/April 2009.

Miège, B. (2010) *L'espace public contemporain, Approche info-communicationnelle*, Presse universitaire de Grenoble.

Taner, T. (2008) *Habermas'ı Okumak (Reading Habermas),* Yordam Kitap.

Verstraeten, H., "The media and the transformation of the public sphere", *European Journal of Communication*, no 11(3), p. 347-370.

# CHAPTER 9

# TRANSPHOBIA IN EBRU NİHAN CELKAN'S KİMSENİN ÖLMEDİĞİ BİR GÜNÜN ERTESİYDİ (AFTER THE DAY NOBODY DIED)[1]

## Evrim Ersöz Koç

*This play is a test of our humanity through a trans woman… (After the Day)*

Since the last decade in both private theater companies and state theater in Turkey, there has been a rise in the number of transgender characters or themes that invite the audience into the hardships the transgender individuals face. Along with the adaptation of "in-yer-face" movement in alternative theater and pride parades that hope for a better integration of LGBTQ into everyday life, transgender characters that previously emerged on the Turkish stages as "stereotypes" has developed into more complex characters that enable a better grasp of their psychological and social traumas in patriarchal heteronormative societies (Baş, 2016; Celkan, 2014; Mitrani, 2014). Celkan comments on this change of transgender individuals on the Turkish stage stating that "their journey from the streets to the stages also encapsulates a journey from "type" to "character" (Celkan, 2014). Among these plays that enrich the Turkish drama with transgender characters are *Cadının Bohçası (The Sack of the Witch)* by Esmeray, *Pembe Gri (Pink Gray)* by Pembe Hayat LGBTT Tiyatro Topluluğu (Pink Life LGBTT Theater Group), *80'lerde Lubunya Olmak (Being a Transsexual in the 80s)* and *90'larda Lubunya Olmak (Being a Transsexual in the 90s)* written by Siyah Pembe Üçgen İzmir Derneği (Black Pink Triangle İzmir Association) and directed by Ufuk Tan Altunkaya, *Garaj (Garage)* by Kemal Hamamcıoğlu, *İz (Trace)* by Ahmet Sami Özbudak and *Kadınlar Aşklar ve Şarkılar (Women Amour and Songs)* by Şamil Yılmaz. As Elif Baş stresses in her article "From Self-Effacement to Confrontation: The

---

[1] Since there is no printed translation of the play *Kimsenin Ölmediği Bir Günün Ertesiydi*, all the quotations from the play (as well as several reviews of the play on Turkish newspapers) are translated by the author of this article.

Emergence of Queer Theatre in Istanbul," a list including LGBT characters "may not be long, but the very airing of such issues on stage has marked an important turning point in Turkish theatre" (2016, p.127).

Ebru Nihan Celkan's play *After the Day Nobody Died* is one of these recent productions in Turkish drama that explores the life of a transgender named Umut. Sumru Yavrucuk insightfully plays Umut in her solo performance which wins her several theater awards[2]. In this "one-man show of a woman" (After the Day), Umut as a transgender sex worker shares not only her present-day experiences with her neighbors, her transgender community, her clients but also past memories with her first love, former clients and most significantly, her parents. All those experiences and memories that highlight the sense of insecurity for a transgender in Turkey reach to a climax at the end that depict Umut being murdered by one of his clients. Through Umut's monologues, the audience is invited into both joy and despair but above all the play provides a striking critique of transphobic heteronormative culture. Following a brief scrutiny on transphobia and related terminology including stigma, genderism and gender bashing, this chapter analyzes how Ebru Nihan Celkan criticizes transphobia through the monologues of a transgender character who is a victim of a hate crime in *After the Day Nobody Died*.

In order to understand the dominant thematic pattern of transphobia in Celkan's play, brief background information about the study on transphobia is necessary. One of the terms that plays a vital role in later studies on homophobia and transphobia is "stigma". Erving Goffman in *Stigma: Notes on the Management of Spoiled Identity* (1963) uses the term stigma in relation with social identity to illustrate how a society categorizes its people. According to Goffman, "the Greeks . . . originated the term stigma to refer to bodily signs designed to expose something unusual and bad about the moral status of the signifier. The signs were cut or burnt into the body and advertised that the bearer was a slave, a criminal, or a traitor—a blemished person, ritually polluted, to be avoided, especially in public places" (1963, p.10). There were two additions to the term in Christian times: bodily signs of holy grace and bodily signs of physical disorder (Goffman, 1963, p.10). Goffman states that "today the term is widely used in something like the original literal sense, but is applied more to the disgrace itself than to the bodily evidence of it" (1963, p.10). Goffman analyzes stigmas under three different types:

*First there are abominations of the body - the various physical deformities. Next there are blemishes of individual character perceived as weak will, domineering or unnatural passions, treacherous and rigid beliefs, and dishonesty, these being inferred from a known record of, for example, mental disorder, imprisonment, addiction, alcoholism,*

---

[2] Among the best actress awards that were presented to Sumru Yavrucuk were the ones given by TEB Tiyatro Ödülleri (Theater Critics Union Awards), Afife Tiyatro Ödülleri (Afife Theater Awards) and Sadri Alışık Tiyatro Ödülleri (Sadri Alışık Theater Awards).

*homosexuality, unemployment, suicidal attempts, and radical political behavior. Finally, there are the tribal stigma of race, nation, and religion, these being stigma that can be transmitted through lineages and equally contaminate all members of a family. (1963, p.13).*

Goffman's analysis of stigma contributed to later scrutiny on sexual stigma (Herek, 2004, 2007; Jones et al, 1984; Link& Phelan, 2001; Plummer 1975). Herek in his article "Beyond 'Homophobia': Thinking about sexual prejudice and stigma in the twenty-first century" summarizes five points about stigma in the present discussion as follows:

*First, stigma refers to an enduring condition or attribute, a physical or figurative mark borne by an individual. Second, the attribute or mark is not inherently meaningful; meanings are attached to it through social interaction. Third, the meaning attached to the mark by the larger group or society involves a negative valuation...*

*A fourth feature of stigma is that it engulfs the entire identity of the person who has it. Stigma does not entail social disapproval of merely one aspect of an individual, as might be the case for an annoying habit or a minor personality flaw. Rather, it trumps all other traits and qualities... Finally, the roles of the stigmatized and normal are not simply complementary or symmetrical. They are differentiated by power. Stigmatized groups have less power and access to resources than do normals. (2004, p.14)*

Thus, Herek emphasizes that stigma which may be either physical or figurative is given a meaning in the social interaction and that the boundaries between the stigmatized and the normal[3] take shapes in power relations. Herek evaluates sexual stigma associating this power relation between the stigmatized and the normal with the hierarchical power relation between homosexual and heterosexual: "in that hierarchy of power and status, homosexuality is devalued and considered inferior to heterosexuality. Homosexual people, their relationships, and their communities are all considered sick, immoral, criminal or, at best, less than optimal in comparison to that which is heterosexual" (2004, p.15)

In the very beginning of this article, Herek stresses two significant events in the early 1970s that contribute to later studies about sexual orientation both in the United States and the rest of the world (2004, p. 6). The first one is the removal of homosexuality from *Diagnostic and Statistical Manual of Mental Disorders* which contributed to a dramatic shift in how homosexuality is regarded (2004, p. 6).[4] The second one is George Weinberg's introduction of

---

[3] Herek states in parenthesis that the term "normal" is Goffman's choice for nonstigmatized (2004, p. 9)

[4] It is so unfortunate that 40 years later than the removal of homosexuality from diagnostic category, Aliye Kavaf, former Minister of State Responsible for Women and Family Affairs, stated in 2010 that "homosexuality is a disease and should be treated." Such a statement unsurprisingly led to a heated response and uproar in Turkey: for instance, Turkish Medical Association called for her resignation since such a statement can trigger homophobia and hate crimes (TTB Etik Kurul, 2010) and The Pink Life Association which is a significant LGBT organization in Turkey asked for her apology and resignation

the term *homophobia* in *Society and the Healthy Homosexual* which "challenged entrenched thinking about the 'problem' of homosexuality (Herek, 2004, p. 6). The invention of the term *homophobia* is, for Herek, a milestone since "it crystallized the experiences of rejection, hostility, and invisibility that homosexual men and women in mid-20th century North America had experienced throughout their lives" (2004, p. 8). Since then, homophobia "has served as a model for conceptualizing a variety of negative attitudes based on sexuality and gender (2004, p. 9) and "has been a tremendously valuable tool for raising society's awareness about the oppression of sexual minorities (2004, pp. 13-14).

One of the terms that is proliferated by the invention of the term of homophobia is certainly transphobia which "entered Western academic discourse as activists in English-speaking trans communities during the 1990s described the hatred and prejudice—sometimes subtle, sometimes not—that transsexual and transgender people experience in everyday life" (Hill, 2016, p. 1272). "Obviously inspired by the term *homophobia*, transphobia came to describe the feelings and thoughts associated with a fear or disgust of trans people" (Hill, 2016, p. 1272). Even though it is true that "while a large amount of literature on homophobia has been produced, transphobia remains an understudied topic" (Bandini & Maggi, 2014, p. 50).

Before extending on transphobia, defining the umbrella term transgender which includes crossdressers or transvestites, transgenderists, transsexuals and intersexuals is essential:

> *Transgender is an identity that has emerged in the past three decades. It refers to people who refuse to live up to society's expectations for gender. It is best understood as a "community" identity used by a collective of people who have personal identities as cross-dressers or transvestites (those who enjoy occasional or recreational crossgender presentations); transgenderists (those who live a substantial part of their lives cross-gender); pre-, post-, and nonoperative transsexuals (those who desire to permanently alter their secondary sexual characteristics so as to live the remainder of their lives cross-gender); and intersexuals (those who have "mixed" genetic, anatomical, or hormonal indications of sex. (Hill, 2002, p. 113)*

To understand anti-transgender violence, one of the terms that is commonly used is transphobia; however, according to Hill, there are two more concepts that conceptualize this violence. Genderism which "is a concept obviously inspired by feminist discourse on sexism" "is the cultural notion that gender is an important basis by which to judge people and that nonbinary genders are anomalies" (Hill, 2002, pp. 118-119). The other concept is gender bashing which "denotes the harassment, abuse, or assault of gender and sex nonconformists" (Hill, 2002, p. 120). Hill sums up these

---

(Bawer, 2010).

three concepts in a comparative view as follows:

*Basically, genderism and transphobia are the attitudes, and gender bashing is the behavior. Genderism provides the negative cultural attitude; transphobia fuels the attitude with fear, disgust, and hatred; and gender bashing is the violent expression of these beliefs. Although genderism and transphobia often result in covert expressions of discrimination and antipathy, gender bashing is an overt expression of hostility. (Hill, 2002, p. 120).*

Celkan's play *After the Day Nobody Died* is a striking critique of genderism, transphobia and gender bashing. The protagonist is named as Umut who is "a 45-years-old woman (transsexual)" (Celkan, 2013, p. 10) and Celkan presents Umut's life story in a fragmentary style. *After the Day Nobody Died* can also be regarded as a memory play because even though the play takes place in one day in Umut's life which she leads as a transgender sex worker in Istanbul, her memories which date back even to her childhood provide a better understanding of the hardships she has endured in a heteronormative society.

In these recollections the hardness of coming to terms with her gender identity for Umut is obvious. This difficulty is first apparent in her dialogue with the janitor's son. Umut loves the child and takes care of him and gives him pocket money all the time. The child also loves Umut and her friends referring to them as sisters. In Umut's memory, the child asks her "who created you" and Umut replies "the one who created you" (Celkan, 2013, p. 13). Then the child offers Umut to teach how to pray and asks "are you a believer?" (Celkan, 2013, p. 13). Umut's answer illustrates how she is engaged with the an idea of a creater/god when she is trying to recognize, reject or make sense of her gender identity in different phases of her life:

*I used to believe little man…In the past I used to pray when I went to bed each night. God please please please fix me. I don't want t be like that. Take those feelings inside me. Please! I don't want to make my mother cry.*

*(Pause.)*

*Then I began to say: God I will never kiss a man. Never never never…*

*(Pause.)*

*It didn't happen (One moment) Why did you create me like that? Why me? I hate you. I HATE YOU!*

*(Pause.)*

*Help me to be a woman. Help me not to get killed somewhere alone. Help my mother to be happy. Help the world. Help the children and the women. If you exist, if you are somewhere out there, for the children and the women… You have to exist for the children and the women. (Celkan, 2013, p. 13)*

In relation with the concept of the creator of humankind, these lines indicate her different responses to her gender identity including the need to feel "normal", denial, rejection and at last self-acceptance. The progressive movement to self-acceptance in her gender identity development also entails a realization of the difficulty of being not only a transgender but also a woman or a child in a patriarchal heterosexist society.

There is a strong sense of genderism which is most potent in her family relations especially with her father. Umut's father, a military officer, is physically abusive towards Umut and Umut is worried whether her father may project violence on to her mother as well. This domestic violence becomes obvious first in Umut's phone call with her mother in which Umut asks her whether she is physically abused by him: "He is not touching you, Right? Just tell me . . . Say that bastard...even if he touches you once...just for once..." (Celkan, 2013, p. 14).

Umut's story is shaped by the feelings towards her parents: love and admiration for the mother and anger towards the father. Umut, whose name means *hope,* says that her mother used to call her "my hope," so Umut is "one and only hope of the most beautiful mother in the world" (Celkan, 2013, p. 21). On the other hand, the only feeling Umut has for the father is outrage which is most explicit in the fight between the two which led her to leave the house when she was at high school. The night the father beat her was also the night when she had her first kiss. She narrates her psychology in those days with her admiration for the popular and successful singer, transgender diva in Turkey named Bülent Ersoy[5]: "on this earth, there is only me and Bülent Ersoy. Two creatures, two extraterrestrial scumbags...I hate myself but I want to live. She managed... If she did, I can too" (Celkan, 2013 p. 21). That night Umut went to a bar with her friends and began flirting with a guy which ended up in her first kiss experience. She explains the joy and happiness that this experience resulted in as "The world stops. There is no one around. An intense silence. The world stops. The world becomes me. The world becomes us. The world exists. Here is the world... here is love. HERE I AM!" (Celkan, 2013, p. 22). When she came home from the bar, there was still makeup on her face which triggered first verbal and later physical abuse. Her father responds: "What is it on your face dick, are you a faggot?" (Celkan, 2013, p. 22). Then comes the line which proves genderism in heterosexist and patriarchal society when her father says "Dou you want to be fucked! You want this son of a bitch. Isn't that enough that I fucked your mother, shall I fuck you as well! (Celkan, 2013, p. 23). This is genderism which rest on the negative evaluation of people based on sex and gender

---

[5] For more information on the significance of Bülent Ersoy as an iconic public figure, see Altınay (2008) and Selen (2012).

conformity (Hill, 2002, pp.118-119) in a very inappropriate and abominable form. As the patriarch in the heteronormative society, he ascribes himself as the powerful figure who can dominate the powerless such as woman (wife) and nonheterosexual (child). From his perspective, sexual intercourse or "fucking" is a power show, a mechanism to rule over the less powerful. Following that horrific sexist verbal abuse, he began beating Umut in spite of her constant pleading not to do so. This is how she left home which she describes as: "that morning I left as a man, that night I entered Istanbul as a woman" (Celkan, 2013, p. 23). Although she left her hometown and goes away from her father, her anger definitely did not disappear. She associates her father with the mold on the wall of the hotel room whenever she goes to Yıldız Hotel to work: "on the head side of the bed, on the wall there is a green damp which looks like my father's ass, we become friends with it… When an immigrant worker or greengrocer in the neighborhood, who knows, is coming back and forth behind me, it seems to me that I am looking at my father's ass and I am delighted…Whenever it hurts, I yell "Fucked bastard" (Celkan, 2013, p. 19). The word "bastard" here does not only refer to the client who is hurting her but also to her father who has traumatized her both physically and psychologically. Through this association with her father and the stinking mold, it is obvious that every form of physical pain is reminiscent of her father.

Later in the play, Umut refers to that traumatic experience of both verbal and physical abuse at her last night home stating that he beat me for being like that despite her constant promises to be different. Moreover, her father is not an exception or a psycho; there is a widespread inclination for physical violence towards transgender individuals which is explicit in her statement as "the men who came into my life after my father beat me anyway" (Celkan, 2013, p. 27). In a heteronormative society, in which heterosexuality is the norm, there are boundaries separating the heterosexuals and nonheterosexuals triggered by power relations and these boundaries justify the violent attitudes imposed on nonheterosexuals from the perspectives of heterosexuals.

At this point, it is wise to remember Herek's scrutiny on sexual stigma in which he uses Goffman's groundbreaking theorization of stigmas in general as a background. As also stated above, Herek outlines five points about stigma the last of which outlines the role of power as a differentiating force between the stigmatized and the "normal" (2004, p. 9). Power plays a significant role in Herek's progression from Goffman's general theorization of stigma to particular consideration of sexual stigma which "refers to the shared knowledge of society's negative regard for any nonheterosexual behavior, identity, relationship, or community" (2004, p. 15).

*The ultimate consequence of sexual stigma is a power differential between heterosexuals and nonheterosexuals. It expresses and perpetuates a set of hierarchical relations within society. In that hierarchy of power and status, homosexuality is devalued and considered inferior to heterosexuality. Homosexual people, their relationships, and their communities are all considered sick, immoral, criminal or, at best, less than optimal in comparison to that which is heterosexual. (Herek, 2004, p. 15)*

The play exactly criticizes the stigmatization of transgender individuals in which they are considered "sick, "immoral" and "criminal." In the very beginning of the play, there is a stigmatization of transgender individuals as "sick." When the janitor's son becomes ill and the janitor takes him to hospital, the doctor's assumption that the kid probably has caught the disease from the faggots is an example of sexual stigma. In the eyes of the heterosexuals, the transgender are stigmatized as "sick" and contagious. In addition, the play includes a pondering on the concept of morality especially in the way Umut talks about her clients. Umut mentions that she did not have sex reassignment surgery since much of her clients ask for being receptive (passive) partners in anal intercourse: "Supply-demand...they come to be fucked. Retired teacher, doctor, cab driver, neighbor, brother Ahmet, Imam of the mosque Uncle Mehmet, the popular, moral and breadwinner artist... Is it there? Come on fuck me...come on my husband" (Celkan, 2013, p. 20). Umut emphasizes the fact that her clients appear as emblems of morality: "soon they will come... the ones who have just arrived at Istanbul, the old ones, tourists...the Pious. The moral. The honorable and dignified shopkeepers. They fuck and go as I look at my father's ass in the midst of the fucked smell of the fucked room" (Celkan, 2013, p. 26). Also, she questions the morality of her last client whose nickname is Orhan the Ox which is evident in her statement as "NO-ONE NO-ONE BECOMES A PROSTITUTE WILLINGLY. Your sense of morality looks like my ass. Tell these lies to your wife and daughter" (Celkan, 2013, p. 27). In a sense, these lines are questioning the hypocrisy and immorality of her clients in the heteronormative society which stigmatize transgender sex workers as "immoral." The last stigma that Herek highlights to be attributed to the nonheterosexuals is "criminal". Umut mentions that whenever a friend of them is killed as a victim of hate crime, they want to take care of the funeral and take care of their friend for the last time, but they are kicked out of the cemetery. The tension in the cemetery is presented in the media with the headlines "they do not even have respect for the funeral," "Again they make a scene" "Again the transvestites cause scandals in the cemetery" (Celkan, 2013, p. 19). Umut wants to stress that all the transvestites (who are stigmatized in the newspapers as criminals) want is to be there for their friends for a final farewell, but they are not welcomed.

In addition to genderism and sexual stigma, the last basis that is related with the thematic exploration of transphobia in this play is the concept of hate crime which may be evaluated as a part of gender bashing. Umut's story strikingly portrays the victimization of transgender individuals as a result of hate crimes. As also emphasized in the title, the play begins "after the day nobody died." The title of the play is also the opening line; Umut wants to celebrate and have *güllüm* ("fun")[6] because nobody in their community died the day before. Umut is anxious that she is late for home because her roommate Ece may panic and run to hospitals or somewhere else to be sure she is okey. This shows that each member of the community is always hesitant and nervous that another one may be in trouble or fall victim to a hate crime. The terror of hate crime lies in the fact that not only transgender individuals are killed but also the ones who manage to survive have to live with the idea that they might be murdered any time. They live constantly in the midst of danger which is obvious in Umut's prayer for not being killed somewhere alone (Celkan, 2013, p. 13). Also Umut mentions about Gülbahar, one of her friends in trans community who was killed at her house. Umut introduces Gülbahar as the oldest one in the community and mourning for her friend, Umut says that "Death does not come. They do not let death visit us, they do it themselves with their own hands. Killing us is like catching flies" (Celkan, 2013, p. 16). Moreover, when she talks about the funerals of her friends, she asks "When will it be my turn?" and then rearticulates "Death does not come and take us" (Celkan, 2013, pp. 18-19). Definitely, the most poignant image related with the cruelty of hate crime is the climactic ending of the play when Umut is murdered by Orhan the Ox who is probably one of the figures in the neighborhood she has acquaintance with. Although Umut is familiar with Orhan the Ox, she makes it clear he has never been her client before. When they are alone, first Umut asks him "do you think it is possible for a human to be born in the wrong body" (Celkan, 2013, p. 26) and then with an explicit reference to body/soul dualism and a remembrance of her last night at her home she reveals that her soul is dead: "My soul… The soul of a human is the mother. My soul…my soul was frozen ten years ago… My soul was first raped and then abandoned in a living room among carved sofas and chat tables that were never used and reserved for the guests" (Celkan, 2013, p. 27). After she states that not only her father but also all the other men that entered her life were abusive towards her, Umut is to live the most violent and also the last experience of her life. Asking for a hundred dollars, first she gives him a blowjob and then makes fun of him first for his desire to be a receptive (passive) partner in anal intercourse and then for early ejaculation. Then she says "don't pull my head" (Celkan, 2013, p. 28). Following a ten seconds blackout on stage, she narrates the moment of her own murder as follows:

*He pulled my head. Then he slid the blunt pocketknife which he bought from a street vendor at Karaköy for three Turkish Liras from right to left on my neck. I saw my blood gushing. It blended into the night. We were to have fun with friends. Today*

---

[6] The idioms "güllüm" "güllüm etmek" which may be translated as "fun" and "having fun" are idioms used in Lubunca which refers to vernacular language used among LGBTQ communities in Turkey. As also seen in other LGBTQ plays, novels or biographies, Celkan provides a Lubunca dictionary at the end of the play.

*nobody among us was dead. A day nobody among us was dead. We were supposed to have güllüm ("fun") … As we wish…*

*Tonight*

*yes*

*tonight, I will go for whomever I like, to a handsome laço ("grown man 20-35 years old") …*

*It was the day after nobody died. (Celkan, 2013, p. 29)*

The play ends the way it begins highlighting the fact that Umut is murdered on a day to celebrate since nobody in their transgender community was dead. It is an unfortunate act that keeps the reader or the audience thinking that there is no single day that a transgender individual does not fall victim to hate crime. Evidently one cannot be sure what has tempted Orhan the Ox to kill Umut: maybe he does not want to leave behind a witness to his relation with a trans sex worker or he is bothered by Umut's mocking approach to his interest in being a receptive partner or early ejaculation which are all taboo sensitivities according to hegemonic masculinity norms or he, as a man in heteronormative patriarchal society, is claiming and ensuring his power over the subordinate transsexual. The tragedy is not centered on Orhan the Ox's motivations but on Umut's death on a day after nobody in the transgender community died leaving the reader and the audience with the sad recognition that each day one of them is murdered. As Bandini and Maggi states "The most shocking expression of transphobia is the murder of hundreds of transgenders across the world, as documented by the latest records of deaths provided by the Transgender Europe network (TGEU) on 12 March, 2013, in the framework of its Trans Murder Monitoring Project" (2014, p. 53). For instance, according to these records "1,123 transgenders were murdered in 57 countries worldwide from January1st, 2008 to December 31st, 2012" which is an underestimated number because "in most countries data on these murders are not recorded systematically" (Bandini and Maggi, 2014, p. 53). Therefore, hate crime which is the most violent form of gender bashing is widespread in all countries even though it is hard to give exact numbers. It is so common to see a hate crime in Turkish newspapers or social media in which a transgender, such as Çağla Joker, Çingene Gül, Esra Ateş and Begüm who were killed either in their houses or a hotel room, falls victim to hate crime. From this perspective, although as a theatrical character Umut is not stereotypical on stage illustrated with complexity and depth (as mentioned in the introduction of this study), her story is unfortunately typical of a transgender individual in any patriarchal heteronormative country.

In the preface to play, Celkan states that "there is only one basis that has been significant for me since the day I submitted the play. 'Umut's story is valuable and people have to know its value…' If the trans-individual Umut's story manages to take attention to hate crime news that has been significant for no one previously, it means that the journey of the play goes well" (Celkan, 2013, p. 7). Thus, Celkan writes the play with a mission—to make people aware of the tragedy of hate crimes and to fight against it. At this point, it would be wise to refer to Hill's comments on reducing transphobia: "this greater understanding of transphobia has led to interventions to combat it. One approach based on intergroup contact theory found that meeting and knowing trans people was associated with less transphobia, so simply listening to a trans person talk about their life could reduce transphobia" (Hill, 2016, pp. 1272-1273). Therefore, Celkan's play can be evaluated as an "intervention to combat" transphobia providing the people with a chance to see how transgender individuals suffer. Sumru Yavrucuk, the actress playing Umut, responds similar to Celkan stating how it could appear as a healing force for transgender individuals. Yavrucuk mentions about two transsexuals who after watching the play stated that the play relieved the pain in their heart which resembled to the pain of a deceased child and comments that now that I heard it, it means everything, there is no need for anything else (Maro, 2012). Asu Maro, the writer who reported Yavrucuk's comments, asks "what more can we expect from a play?" (Maro, 2012). Therefore, the play combats with transphobia from two bases; to heal and ease the pain of transgender individuals who are subject to cruel forms of stigmatization, genderism and gender bashing and to make other people familiar with their sorrows, worries and alienation in heteronormative society.

To sum up, Celkan's play *After the Day Nobody Died* is one of these recent productions that depict non-stereotypical transgender characters on the Turkish stage. The play presents Umut's last day as a transgender sex worker in Istanbul; however, through her memories the play enables us to make a journey in her past explicating how she makes sense of her gender identity, her relations with her family, her transgender community, her first kiss, the people in the neighborhood, her clients, etc. This journey provides a better understanding of the worries, sorrows and sufferings of transgender individuals who are generally stigmatized as "sick" "immoral" and "criminal" and are subject to certain cruel forms of genderism in transpobic society. The play which is an impressive critique of stigmatization, genderism and gender bashing, makes it evident how the prevalence of hate crimes leads transgender individuals to a sense of insecurity even if they manage to survive. Hopefully, the play manages to heal transgender individuals who face isolation, rejection and hate in heteronormative societies and to make other people aware of the ills of transphobia. Thereby, Umut's story can bring a glimpse of "hope" for a better society even though she falls victim to a hate crime in *After the Nobody Died*.

# REFERENCES

After the Day Nobody Died. *Altıdan Sonra Tiyatro / Altıdan Sonra Production*. Retrieved from http://www.altidansonra.com/after-the-day-nobody-died.html

Altınay, R. E. (2008). Reconstructing the transgendered self as a Muslim, nationalist, upper-class woman: the case of Bulent Ersoy. *Women's Studies Quarterly*, 36(3/4), 210-229.

Bandini, E., & Maggi, M. (2014). Transphobia. In G. Corono, E. Jannini, & M. Maggi (Eds.), *Emotional, physical, and sexual abuse: Impact in children and social minorities* (pp. 49–70). New York, NY: Springer.

Baş, E. (2016). From self-effacement to confrontation: The emergence of Queer theater in Istanbul. *Asian Culture and History*, 8(2), 126-134.

Bawer, Ç. (2010, Mar. 15). LGBT Association Sues State Minister. *Bianet*. Retrieved from http://bianet.org/kadin/minorities/120658-lgbt-association-sues-state-minister

Celkan, E. N. (2013). Kimsenin Ölmediği Bir Günün Ertesiydi (After the Day Nobody Died). İstanbul, Mitos.

_____ (2014, July 04) Sokaktan sahneye, sahneden sokağa. *Agos*. Retrieved from http://www.agos.com.tr/tr/yazi/7500/sokaktan-sahneye-sahneden-sokaga

Goffman, E. (1963). Stigma: Notes on the management of spoiled Identity. London: Penguin.

Herek, G. M. (2004). Beyond "Homophobia": Thinking about sexual prejudice and stigma in the twenty-first century. *Sexuality Research & Social Policy* 1(2), 6-24.

_____ (2007). Confronting sexual stigma and prejudice: Theory and practice. *Journal of Social Issues* 63 (4), 905-925.

Hill, D. B. (2002). Genderism, transphobia, and genderbashing: A framework for interpreting anti-transgender violence. In B. Wallace & R. Carter (Eds.), *Understanding and dealing with violence: A multicultural approach* (pp. 113–136). Thousand Oaks, CA: Sage.

_____ (2016). Transphobia. In A. E. Goldberg (Ed.), *The Sage encyclopedia of LGBTQ studies* (pp. 1272-1273). Thousand Oaks: Sage.

Jones, E.E., Farina, A., Hastorf, A.H., Markus, H., Miller, D.T., & Scott, R.A. (1984). *Social stigma: The psychology of marked relationships*. New York: W. H. Freeman.

Link, B.G., & Phelan, J.C. (2001). Conceptualizing stigma. *Annual Review of Sociology, 27*, 363-385.

Maro, A. (2012, Dec. 25). "Yüreğimdeki Acıyı Hafiflettin." *Milliyet*. Retrieved from http://www.milliyet.com.tr/yazarlar/asu-maro/-yuregimdeki-aciyi-hafiflettin--1646369/

Mitrani, E. (2014, Jan. 8) "Sahnelerimizi Lubunyalar bastı." *Şalom*. Retrieved from. http://www.salom.com.tr/haber-89619-sahnelerimizi_lubunyalar_basti.html

Plummer, K. (1975). Sexual Stigma: An Interactionist Account. London: Routledge & Kegan Paul.

Selen, E. (2012). The stage for queer subjectification in contemporary Turkey. *Gender, Place & Culture*, 19 (6), 730-749.

TTB Etik Kurul (Ethics Committee of Turkish Medical Association). (2010, May 05). Bakan A. Kavaf'ın 'eşcinselliğin hastalık olduğu' beyanı üzerine görüş. Retrieved from http://www.ttb.org.tr/makale_goster.php?Guid=f7936c66-923f-11e7-b66d-1540034f819c.

.

www.ingramcontent.com/pod-product-compliance
Lightning Source LLC
Chambersburg PA
CBHW030851270326
41928CB00008B/1329